Also by Michael Graham

Banned From Public Radio

Clinton & Me

*How eight years of a
pants-free presidency changed my
nation, my family and my life.*

by

Michael Graham

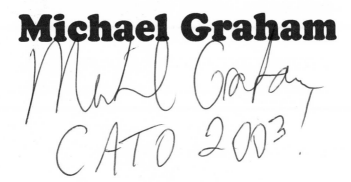

Pinpoint Press
Columbia, S.C.

To my Menckens:

H.L., the greatest American newspaperman of the 20th century, who revealed the secrets of Clintonism more than 50 years ago: "Democracy is the theory that the common people know what they want and deserve to get it...good and hard";

And to my eldest son, Mencken Powell Graham, who showed up just in time to see all the fun.

Acknowledgments

This book simply would not have been possible without the help of:

Amy, John, Noel, Stephanie, Margaret and the other publishers and editors who have shown tremendously poor judgment by publishing my work;

Randall, who gave me my first job in talk radio and has been trying unsuccessfully to get me to shut up ever since;

Colin at Warner Books who, along with Richard, Mary, Pete, Janna, Oran and (especially) J. Mark, offered timely advice on the contents herein;

John, my fellow curmudgeon, who got this whole mess started with the seemingly innocent comment, "Hey, you ever thought about writing a book?";

But most of all, my wife, Jennifer, aka "The Warden," a wonderful mother, a skilled copyeditor, an outstanding grammarian and one hot [*deleted on final edit*].

This book is entirely their fault. Like the president, I accept no responsibility whatsoever.

Contents

Preface

How Bill Clinton Changed My Life

God, I'm going to miss him.

I, Michael Graham, a southern-born, right-wing, pro-life, school-choice, Second-Amendment, abstinence-based, laissez-faire, Laffer-curve, "let them eat cake" Reagan Republican of the first order, would be willing to suspend the Constitution just to keep Bill Clinton around.

In 1992, when Clinton and his saxophone burst on the American scene, I proudly cast my vote against him. Now that the Clinton show is tentatively scheduled to close January 20, 2001 (with this guy, you never know), I can hardly bear to see him go.

For starters, he's not Al Gore. Al Gore -- who combines the politics of Ralph Nader with the ethics of Richard Nixon -- has all the venal ambition and grating self-righteousness of Bill Clinton, but with none of the offsetting charm.

Watching Al Gore campaign for president is like watching a teen-aged boy trying to get laid: He's working so hard, and he wants it so bad, but you're not sure anybody's going to enjoy it much if he actually gets the chance.

With President Clinton, it's the opposite: You know you're going to enjoy it; you're just not sure you should.

I've enjoyed the Clinton presidency thoroughly, and for so many different reasons. It's been great for me economically, and I don't mean that in the Clinton "I Single-Handedly Rescued the Economy From Ronald Reagan's Eight Straight Years of Economic Growth" sense of the phrase. I literally owe my career (such as it is) as a former political operative and current columnist and talk show host to the Clinton administration. And I am confident there are thousands of other Americans (Internet gossips, IRS investigators, chastity-belt manufacturers) who can say the same thing.

What better time to be in the business of political conversation than when the hottest media star in the nation lives at 1600 Pennsylvania Avenue? How lucky am I to have a president who turns me into a successful humorist every time I merely quote him accurately?

And Bill Clinton single-handedly made me a radio talk show host. My first night on the air was the same night the Washington Post broke the Monica story.

Yes, Virginia, there is a Santa...

Before Bill Clinton, talk hosts spent hours trying to find ways to make the inner workings of democracy interesting to the average American. My first week in talk radio, my listeners and I spent hours trying to find polite ways to describe what Monica Lewinsky was doing under the President's desk (First runner-up: "face time." Winner: "Hailing the Little Chief.")

Bill Clinton forever answered the question, "How do you get Americans engaged in their political system?" Answer: Drop your pants!

My fellow conservatives and I have had a great time pounding the president over his cigar-handling antics. But I don't think my fellow conservatives fully appreciate how much Bill Clinton has done for our cause.

I remember a conversation back in the Reagan years, when I was living in New York City. I was talking to a moderate NYC Democrat (he was a Marxist) about why I distrusted government. "Absolute power corrupts absolutely! The government which governs best, governs least! Fight the power!"

He was unimpressed. "Government isn't any worse than big business or anyone else," he insisted. "I've never seen politicians act as corrupt or selfish or power-hungry as you keep saying they do."

I hope he's been paying attention.

We conservatives should thank Bill Clinton for demonstrating in real life the kind of shameless, petty abuses of power that before we could only describe. Never again will mainstream Americans be able to say, "No president would ever do THAT!" Think about it: Can you think of anything, literally anything, that this president would not do for the sake of his own political success?

I have written, in print and for broad publication, that if it would help him achieve his political ends, Bill Clinton would announce tomorrow that he is a lesbian.

I further maintain that 43 percent of the American voting public would believe him.

In the past, I might have written columns warning of a president's theoretical use of the FBI and the IRS to pursue his enemies; or a parody of a president so desperate for campaign funds that he invited agents of Communist China over for tea; or a tribute to George Orwell suggesting that some politicians might not be sure of the definition of the word "is."

Before President Clinton, all this would have been comedy. Today, it is history.

One last, personal note: Bill Clinton has had a real impact on my marriage. One can only speculate how many husbands of Arkansas state employees can make that same claim.

Like most men in their 30s, I've cavalierly spouted the nostrum "All men are pigs." And for the most part, we are. But there is, deep inside us, some notion of - for lack of a better phrase - pig's pride.

Do I know guys who've engaged in extramarital knee grabbing? Do I know bosses who give their attractive female assistants a few laps around the desk whenever possible? Of course. I know men like these because I know men.

But part of that view of manhood is the attendant sense of shame. The guys who break their vows and get caught understand that they are the bad guys. They're ashamed of themselves, ashamed of what they've done and, most of all, ashamed of shaming their families.

If I were President Clinton and I had been caught playing "Hide The Cuban" with the office help -- added to all the other leacheries now on the public record -- there would have been no Starr investigation or impeachment proceedings or eye-rolling defenses by Jim Carville.

I would have been gone. Forget the law, as Monica's ex-attorney might say. I would not have had the ego and arrogance to shame my family and show up for work the next day.

I know people make mistakes, and I am certainly not perfect. Knowing the way life goes, I fully anticipate reading the headline "S.C. Commentator Caught With Goat In Cheap Motel" sometime after the publication of this book.

But I can say with all honesty that I have a deeper sense of the value of commitment and a clearer understanding of the importance of my family, all thanks to Bill Clinton. How's that for family values?

After eight years of Bill Clinton, the credibility of government is lower, my personal income is higher, and my family is stronger than ever. Plus, I know 17 new euphemisms for oral sex.

Damn, I am going to miss this guy.

C h a p t e r 1

"Don't Stop Thinking About Tomorrow"

Clinton & Me

January, 1994

One year ago, the same week William Jefferson Clinton was sworn in as head of our national family, I became a father. I'm not sure which one of us was more nervous, but there were probably more pictures taken of me than of him that week.

While the President stood in the chilling January wind and delivered his inaugural address, I paced across a cold hospital floor with my newly delivered son, Mencken. As the President prayed for wisdom and strength to lead our nation, I prayed, too...prayed I wouldn't drop him, that the odor seeping from his diaper was just gas, that he wouldn't grow up to appear on a TV talk show ("Psycho Killers and the Parents Who Raise Them -- next on Jerry Springer.").

As is the case with President Clinton, most of the credit for my achievement must go to the dogged determination of my wife, who was promoting my rise to fatherhood by dumping her birth-control products down the toilet while I wasn't looking.

Behind every great man...

1

Also like the President, I was an unlikely nominee for my new leadership position. I had no previous experience, and I was hardly the consensus candidate of my wife's family. Then there was the character issue. I have none. I am notoriously irresponsible, immature and negligent. I once had a Chia Pet taken into protective custody by the SPCA.

Add to that my lifelong dislike of children. I have always found their sounds, their voices, their very presence, unbearable. Like W.C. Fields, I have long been admired for my hatred of dogs and babies: "Children," I used to note, "should be *steamed*, not heard. And served with drawn butter."

Were it not for my innate "Bobbittophobia," I would have had a vasectomy long ago.

A poll of friends and family would have put the odds of my being a father about the same as Michael Jackson being named spokesman for Underoos. Or of an unknown Arkansas politico with an aversion to military service and a taste for coed slumber parties becoming Commander-In-Chief.

Nevertheless, in our first year, President Clinton and I approached the daunting tasks at hand with enthusiasm, if not competence. While the White House struggled to put together a cabinet, I discovered I had an ex-officio child-rearing "kitchen cabinet" consisting of every female relative and/or co-worker my wife has ever known. While the President was distancing himself from long-forgotten fiascos like Zoë Baird and Kimba Wood, I was trying to figure out how to get their tax-free nannies to move to South Carolina.

And as the President signed the "Family Leave Bill," guaranteeing all loving parents the right to stay home with the little one, my wife was screaming: "If you think I'm staying trapped in this house with that 20-decibel drool machine, you're out of your mind!"

As the President's poll numbers dropped, so did my confidence. Maybe I wasn't the right man for the job. With household deficits rising due to the sudden surge in spending by the "Dept. of Diapers and Bizarre Rash Ointments," I barely managed to push through my own budget proposal. Victory was assured only after a hefty increase in the "Anyone Who Has Worn The Same Smock For 9 Months Deserves All The New Clothes She Wants" Fund.

But we stumbled forward, Clinton and me. Through the hot summer and the fading fall, the President and I refused to quit. Sure, there were embarrassing moments for both of us -- fortunately, I don't have any Janet "Fireball" Renos to answer for.

President Clinton pushed past Ross Perot to get NAFTA, and I got Mencken to sleep through the night, proving we could both effectively handle baldish, goofy-looking whiners with big ears. Then came GATT and big fourth-quarter growth numbers and drinking from a cup and my first solo baby bath (no fatalities), and at the end of year one, it looks like things are turning around.

Are they? Who knows? The economy and children are both very resilient. It could be that they would flourish with or without our guidance. They are also very fickle, and the healthy growth of a well-fed youngster can quickly turn into the pitiful cry of a croupy child. We can only hope for the best.

So happy birthday, Mencken Graham, and congratulations on your first year, Mr. President. I was with you all the way.

Oh, and have you heard about the terrible twos?

They Say It's Your Birthday

February, 1996

In a few days, I will be as old as Jesus.

Our Lord and Savior survived 33 years on this accursed sphere before the locals finally did him in (an ever-present reminder of why I oppose the death penalty, by the way). And this week I will turn 33, which I've just discovered is "The Age."

There is, I believe, for each of us, the one birthday we truly dread. It is the year by which we should have arrived, the date after which there can be no beginnings. It is a boundary marked in our biological clocks, the beginning of the end.

According to Hallmark card mythology, the "C'est Fini" season is 40. You see it almost every day in the paper. The gang at the office chips in for a surprise ad on your 40th birthday. You wake up in a foul mood, open the sports section and there's a quarter-page print of your high-school yearbook photo -- an Opie-look-alike with "Lordy, Lordy, look who's Forty!" in large type underneath.

If any of my so-called friends ever did this to me, by the way, I'd give them a thorough prostate exam with the Sunday "Parade" section.

What's interesting is how most of the people I know who've hit 40 seem to have taken it in stride. Most of them tell me that the 30th birthday was tougher, or that 60 looks rough. The forties actually get pretty good reviews from survivors, some of whom even say life begins there. H.L. Mencken said, "The best years are the forties; after fifty a man begins to deteriorate, but in the forties he is at the maximum of his villainy."

I can hardly wait.

Forty has gotten bad press because it serves as the portal of "middle age," when you've supposedly reached the apogee of your lifeline and have fewer miles out your windshield than in your rear-view mirror.

But since when is 40 middle age? How many people do you know who make it to 80? Unless your last name is Thurmond, middle age hits most of us in our mid-to-late thirties...which means it's sneaking up on me right now.

But I don't see a connection between "The Age" and the end. Indeed, I've known people who have hit "The Age" as old as 60 and as young as 16. It's not death we fear -- it's inconsequence. The bad year is the year when you believe you should have arrived, but didn't.

See, I have a notion in the cramped closets of my psyche that by the age of 33, a young man (or woman) should have done something significant: climbed a mountain, made a million, died on a cross for the sins of the world.

Nothing major, just something to solidify one's career track.

For me, it's 33. But I've heard college students sit at a bar and berate themselves: "I'm 21, and what have I done with my life?" they groan. Telling them the answer ("Drank beer, partied and learned all the lyrics to the 'Brady Bunch' theme song") doesn't seem to help. Get out the Geritol: it's already too late.

As the dreaded day drifts closer, so do my own questions. What have I accomplished? Have I finally "grown up?" How did I turn out this way and who can I sue?

In fact, I've actually done one of the things I swore I would do before 33: I wrote a book. Interestingly, it didn't happen until late last year, just under the wire. I've wondered if the pressure of my self-programmed deadline helped me to finally cut through the psychobabble and get it done. If so, then perhaps this "Day of Doom" isn't such a bad thing.

But I still dread it. This is the first time since I got rid of my fake I.D. from high school that I've been an age that I didn't want other people to know. I'm old enough now for my age to begin morphing in my mind from a specific numeral to a euphemistic range--"the early thirties," or "thirty-something." It is the beginning of self-deception. It is the beginning of the end.

My best friend in high school once told me that the saddest day of his life was graduation. We went to a small, rural school where he was a big fish in the small, redneck pond. The supply of non-chew-consuming males was unusually small, which artificially inflated his market price among his female peers. All through high school, my friend was popular, admired and as close to the top of the social food chain as he was likely to get. And he knew it.

And, he now admits, his life has never crested as high since. He's not miserable; in fact, he's got a nice life: good job, an attractive wife, some kids -- he's doing fine, really.

Just don't play Springsteen's "Glory Days" around him unless you've got a box of Kleenex and a six-pack.

As for my own encounter with "The Age," well, I can't imagine sitting around next week going, "Oh, if only I were 32 again..." I assume I'll swim through this silly, emotional eddy and get on with life. OK, so I haven't composed an opera or been found in flagrante delicto with the Swedish bikini team. Chances are, my birthday will never be a recognized state holiday. But, hey -- I can handle it. I'm a big boy.

Now, where did I put that Springsteen tape...

Justice Under The Dashboard Lights

March, 1996

From the newswires: A sharply divided Supreme Court ruled Monday against a woman who protested when local authorities seized a car owned by her and her husband after he had sex in it with a prostitute.

Tina Bennis argued that confiscation of the 1977 Pontiac under a Michigan nuisance abatement law violated her constitutional right to due process and represented an unconstitutional taking of her property. But the high court, in a 5-4 opinion by Chief Justice William Rehnquist, upheld the forfeiture as constitutional.

* * *

It must have been the phone call from hell.

"Tina? Tina, honey, it's me. Yeah, I'm down at the police station -- no, no, I'm O.K., uh, well...I'm kind of under arrest. What for? Um, well, for soliciting a hooker -- Honey! Honey, calm down.

"It's all just a misunderstanding, I swear. I pulled over to give a young lady some directions and she got in our car to look at a map and, umm, her contact lens popped out and landed on my zipper and, well, naturally she didn't want it to get all dried out so she picked it up with her tongue...

"Honey, please stop screaming. We can talk about this later, just come pick me up. Whaddaya mean, 'I have the car?' Oh, yeah. Our car. Honey, you're not going to believe this..."

Tina Bennis has the dubious distinction of going down in posterity (unlike her husband's new friend, who did so in a Pontiac) with her name on a Supreme Court case that I believe will long be referenced in American law schools. Like Roe, Plessy and Dred Scott, Ms. Bennis will be forever linked to a really stupid Supreme Court decision.

Clinton and Me

Now, stupid conclusions by the U.S. Supreme Court are nothing new. These are the same bozos who declared the death penalty "unconstitutional" despite the fact that capital punishment is specifically mentioned in the Constitution itself.

The Supreme Court is in the habit of making up the law as it goes along, and most of its off-the-cuff lawmaking you should, as a good American, feel free to ignore. But this time you need to pay attention.

You should pay particular attention if you are a casual drug user, occasional overdrinker or a client of your neighborhood "sex professionals" (as they are known in federally funded research studies.) More and more law enforcement agencies want to take away your stuff if you are caught being naughty in any of the aforementioned manners, and the Supreme Court of the United States says it's fine with them.

Indeed, you don't even have to be a crook. You just have to let someone naughty use your car or crash on your couch, and you, too, could soon see your home auctioned off to the local sheriff.

That's what happened to Ms. Bennis. She and her husband bought a car together for $600. He later used that car without her knowledge to cruise for "pretty women" -- the cash-in-advance kind. She didn't participate in the crime, but she lost her only means of transportation because she "recklessly" allowed her husband to drive under the influence of testosterone.

Knowing she would likely never get her car back, all Ms. Bennis asked for was her share of the confiscated value: $300. Sounds reasonable. After all, what did she do wrong, other than marry a loser?

Sorry, Tina, says the Supreme Court. Tough luck. Hasta la vista, baby. Tina's psychic powers should have revealed that her husband had something burning a hole in his pocket besides that twenty bucks, and she should have stopped him. Because she didn't, Tina Bennis is taking the bus.

8

What does this mean for you, dear reader? Let's say an old high school buddy comes through town and spends the night at your house. He's upstairs smokin' a doobie, and the cops kick in the door. Find a warm grate, pal; you're on the street.

I'm deadly serious. The Supreme Court has ruled that the state can confiscate your property any time -- without due process -- if your stuff is used in a crime. If drugs are involved, they don't even have to prove an actual crime! They can seize property suspected of being used in a drug crime, then force you to come to court and prove that it wasn't.

I have no personal experience with illicit drugs whatsoever (I snorted some Midol once; not much of a buzz, but once a month I have a flashback) and have no sympathy for the hemp crowd. But if I have to choose between a society overrun by horny, stoned street cruisers, or nine jack-boot justices ready to seize my property if I eat a poppy seed bagel, I'll take the passionate potheads. They are less of a risk to my liberty.

And if I'm ever driving through Detroit, Tina Bennis can always get a lift from me. She tried to do us all a favor by taking this case to the Supreme Court to protect us from dumb cops and dumber laws. Unfortunately, as Lenny Bruce observed, "In the Halls of Justice, the only justice is in the halls."

Believe It Or Not

April, 1996

"I don't care to belong to a club that accepts people like me as members."--Groucho Marx.

As a hot-blooded evangelical teen-ager in the South, I grew up hating Catholics.

Interestingly, now that I am an infidel condemned to eternal damnation, I find that I hold the Catholic Church in high regard. Being the preferred faith of a practicing social Darwinist may not spin the Pope's beanie, but it is true nevertheless.

Of the many elements of Catholicism I admire (a clergy that can drink me under the table being but one), I am particularly enamored with its advocacy of discrimination.

I realize that, in the Age of Clinton, the only remaining evil is the sin of calling one's neighbor a sinner. I further acknowledge that the Catholic Church is hardly alone among organized religions in condemning heretics like myself to an eternity in Satan's Crockpot.

But it is only Catholicism that is under siege by sinners demanding to be let in.

Hardly a week goes by without some homosexual group flinging condoms at the neighborhood cathedral because the Church won't let Larry, Darryl and Darryl get married. Then there is the annual media hoohaw when some loose cannon former bishop ordains a married priest, or a female priest -- or even priests married to fellow priests -- all of whom insist that they are, in fact, "good Catholics."

The most recent action is in Italy, where the Vatican is actively opposing gay rights legislation in upcoming elections.

10

"It's anti-gay racism [sic!] pure and simple," says Franco Grillini, an Italian homosexual activist and my nominee for this year's Dan Quayle Word Master award. What's next -- "anti-vegetarian sexism?"

The papists, much to their credit, are unmoved. Despite public pressure, they maintain that homosexuality is a sin. Amid whining from Shannon Faulkner wannabes, they forbid female priests and continue their single-gender policies. In short, with the raging winds of egalitarianism and political correctness buffeting from all sides, the Catholic Church calmly states that it is right and we are wrong. Period.

Now, that's what I call a religion.

Are they right? Who knows. The point is that they truly believe what they preach and, to their credit, act like it. Who wants some weaseley religion where the rules are made up from week to week based on public opinion polls, where people sit around deciding what's right and wrong based on what "feels good?"

That's not a church. That's the Democratic National Committee.

The entire theory of "metaphysics" is that there is knowledge beyond our physical senses. If you truly believe this, then no amount of science or reasoning can (or should) sway you in the least. True believers look down upon the protesting heathens and laugh.

Laughing aside, that's what's happening right now in Nebraska. A Roman Catholic bishop there is giving his members until May 15 to drop their memberships in groups like Planned Parenthood and the Hemlock Society, which openly promote abortion and euthanasia.

Folks, we're not talking about sneaking a Sloppy Joe on Good Friday -- these are pretty big issues. Action by the church seems hardly a surprise.

But it is, especially to Randy Moody, a Catholic who serves on the board of Planned Parenthood of Lincoln, Ne. "I challenge them to excommunicate me," he said. "This may end up in some court if they would proceed to do that."

Yeah! What right does the church have to tell you how to live your life? Who does the Pope think he is, anyway?

To which "court" Mr. Moody might petition remains unknown. Indeed, the question illuminates the core issue that Catholic protesters seem unable to grasp. There is no court. It's God. It's the Bible. That's the deal. There is no ambiguity in the Holy Scriptures on cheatin', stealin' or two-man interior decoratin'. If you don't like the Catholic deal, then try another one: Hindu or Mormon or Amway.

Trust me, no matter how bizarre your thinking or irrational your beliefs, there is someone out there with an offering plate and a cable TV show who will welcome you with open arms.

The whole notion of protesting, suing and assaulting your own religion is inherently nonsensical. If you don't agree with massive chunks of Catholic doctrine, why would you want to be Catholic? If you are pro-abortion and pro-suicide, if you want women clergy and think homosexuality is just fine with the Big Man (Person) upstairs, if you don't think the Bible is true and don't like the Pope's new album, then why not just *leave?* Just turn Methodist or join N.O.W. and get on with your life!

One day the lawyers will figure out some way to force the Catholic Church to abide by the same admissions standards currently used at public universities. When that day comes, the pews will be awash in barely literate (but non-judgmental) parishioners all hoping St. Peter grades on the curve. But until then, this southern boy is cheering for the Whore of Babylon all the way.

Teacher's Pet

January, 1996

Robert "Bubba" Walenski has long been one of the most popular teachers at Dennis-Yarmouth (Ma.) Regional High School.

Bubba is "a freewheeling teacher who let students call him by his first name and taught poetry with rock music," according to the AP. Locals describe him as "a typical '60s prodigy" and "a nice guy that all the kids liked." Indeed, students literally line up for his "Musical Poetry" class to study lyrics by rock stars such as Jim Morrison.

Oh, yeah, I almost forgot: Bubba Walenski makes dirty movies, too.

About 100 of them in his career as a pornographer, according to the Boston Globe. Then again, what do you expect from the one guy in the state of Massachusetts whose nickname is "Bubba?"

I used the word "career," but porn was merely an avocation. Bubba's true life's work is the 20 years he's spent as a high school English teacher.

The skin flicks, well, they're just to pump up his income. Teachers often work second jobs in the summer, and as an instructor of literature, it makes perfect sense for Bubba to be drawn toward the arts. That his films appear on video store shelves next to "Nancy and Her Naughty Nurses" or "On Golden Blonde" is merely a sign of our society's puritan and parochial attitude toward the avant-garde.

If you could only see things from Bubba's angle...that angle being (in one video, at least) from the vantage point of a woman's buttocks, as Walenski sucked her toes and commented wryly, "Boys will be boys!" Bubba would know. He hangs out with them at a public school every day.

As you might expect, Bubba -- the literary pioneer that he is -- has suffered for his art. When a local reporter sniffed out his cinematic sideline out, Bubba was promptly suspended from his teaching job by the school superintendent.

This punitive action sparked an equal and opposite reaction from the usual suspects. The teacher's union (which would demand Charles Manson's release if he had tenure) called Walenski "a very well-respected member of our profession." A former student told the local papers, "I don't think they should fire him.... I don't think he was a pervert."

What the minimum pervert requirements might be in Massachusetts, I can't say, but producing 100 porno videos in your spare time is going to raise a few eyebrows, even in Barney Frank country. The school administration thinks teachers ought to set some kind of "example" and claim that educators should uphold some vague set of "standards." Even a few parents were less than enthusiastic about their daughters spending an hour a day in close quarters with "Butt-rubbin' Bubba."

However muddled the community reaction, the students of Dennis-Yarmouth High spoke clearly, loudly and with one voice: "Bring Back Bubba!" Signs to this effect hung from trees and school buildings as students protested his dismissal. Young people packed a news conference to show their support and bemoan the small-minded notion of the superintendent that Bubba displayed "conduct unbecoming a teacher."

"We love Bubba!" the students shouted. One high school girl told reporters: "It's all crazy. It's really hard for kids to find teachers they like."

She has a point. I've never met Bubba Walenski, but I bet he is the most popular educator in the entire state of Massachusetts. And why wouldn't he be? A hippie high school teacher who goes by "Bubba," plays rock music in class and makes porno movies? This guy is a sophomore's dream come true!

It's always been this way. There are those teachers who "make learning fun," who leave their Shakespeare texts unread and rent the Kenneth Branaugh video instead. They eschew lectures, turning their classes into rap sessions ala Oprah Winfrey or, if possible, Jerry Springer. These are the teachers students love.

Then there are those instructors who insist that their students actually learn. These are the teachers who leave the television off, who refuse to spend any class time at all on the lyric development of Snoop Doggy Dogg.

They regularly find rotten eggs in their desk drawers.

Firing Bubba from his teaching job because of how he spends his weekends may be unconstitutional, but he should be fired nonetheless. There is no doubt that he is guilty of "conduct unbecoming a teacher."

In a nation where high schoolers think logarithms are used in reggae music and believe the Vietnam War was ended by protestors led by Tom Cruise, any teacher who wastes class time on the nuances of "Light My Fire" should be summarily dismissed. Any teacher who is popular with his students should be thoroughly investigated.

If they are male, over 40 and have a ponytail, they should be shot on sight.

No one in America wants to admit this, but learning is hard. It is boring. It is tedious. Being competent is the reward, and learning is the investment. Teachers who "make teaching fun" are as useful as preachers who "make hell happy" or surgeons who "make stitches loose."

Feminist sociologists claim that pornography is inherently damaging to society. But if Bubba Walenski must be loved by someone, I would prefer it be by paid professionals on camera, not public school kids in the classroom. He'll do less damage to society that way.

15

My Grandpa, The Nazi

February, 1996

My grandfather is an FDR, JFK, AFL-CIO, yellow-dog Democrat. His politics were born in the Oklahoma Dust Bowl, hardened under fire on the battlefields of France and set in stone during the post-War labor movement.

And he likes Pat Buchanan.

My grandfather agrees with Pat on all the big stuff. A longtime union activist in southern California, he thinks we make it too easy to import foreign goods and export American jobs. He thinks it's ridiculous that America can't control its own borders, and while living in Los Angeles, he saw first-hand the real-life effects of illegal immigration on wages, taxes and crime. On social issues, Grandpa is less doctrinaire than Patrick J., but the idea that he -- an Okie who fought West Coast bigotry as a youth -- would have to stand in a "quota line" to get a job is unthinkable.

Oh, there's much about Pat Buchanan he doesn't like, particularly that part where Pat calls himself a Republican (a word my grandfather rarely utters unless preceded by a prayerful invocation of God's damnation). But even though his motto is "Better R.I.P Than GOP," my grandfather believes Pat Buchanan has some worthwhile ideas. Buchanan is addressing issues my grandpa cares about; he's promoting a vision of America my grandfather can understand, and, in many cases, support.

Imagine my grandfather's surprise to discover he has become a Nazi.

Now, my grandpa knows Nazis. He saw quite a few of them in World War II -- mostly down the barrel of a rifle. Listening to the Chernobylic reaction to Pat Buchanan coming from the media mainstream, Grandpa has begun to wonder if the Panzers aren't pushing toward our borders at this very minute.

16

Clinton and Me

In the past two weeks, Pat Buchanan has been called every insulting label I've ever heard used to describe a politician: Hitler, racist, sexist, fascist, anarchist, and -- believe it or not -- liberal. The editorial page panic is so complete that a newspaper labeling him "Mussolini Made in America" seemed to be softening its position. Columnists are rolling through a veritable Right-Wing Roget's of famous dictators, from "Patrick Pinochet" to "The Idi Amin of the American Right."

These labels -- hilarious in their hysteria but angering in their arrogance -- are applied with equal venom by Republican and Democrat, liberal and conservative. Even limp-wristed commentators who once lacked the courage to denounce Louis Farrakhan have suddenly grown "cultural cojones." They've filled their public comments with language violent enough to start a fistfight at an Amish wedding.

Watching, reading and listening is my grandfather.

He listens as Buchanan's immigration policy is described as "fascist" and wonders why. After all, Pat Buchanan opposes illegal immigration (do his detractors support it?) and wants to temporarily end legal immigration. We currently have limited immigration, by the way, under a plan enforced by the Clinton administration. So, where's the editorial cartoon of a goose-stepping Hillary?

Now, you may not agree with Buchanan's approach (I don't), but how is it racist? It's not like Pat wants to end immigration to everyone except Norwegian virgins or members of the Von Trapp family. His plan affects England and Ireland the same as Ethiopia and India. He may be right, he may be wrong. But a Nazi?

And, my grandfather wants to know, what is so evil about Buchanan's trade policy? Once again, Buchanan's plan is nothing novel. He believes America should have a different deal with developed nations like Canada, Germany and Japan than we do for lesser-developed, lower-wages nations like Mexico, Poland and China. This is radical? This is extreme?

17

If so, then Ronald Reagan and Bill Clinton are extremists. We already have a Byzantine collection of tariffs, quotas and trade incentives that differ from country to country. If Buchanan were proposing to only trade with "our Aryan brothers" or if he wanted to ban trade with any nation whose name started with a "B," I would understand the anger.

I am a devout free-trader who thinks Pat's policies would be an economic disaster, but I'm not mad at him about it, any more than I'm mad at Ralph Nader or Ross Perot. The intemperance, intolerance and downright nastiness of the attack on Buchanan is mystifying.

It is also dangerous. The double-barreled media attack on Pat Buchanan spreads its shot onto the earnest Americans who hear Buchanan giving voice to the questions and concerns they struggle with every day. These are people like my grandfather, people who -- like Buchanan -- may be right or wrong, but who are asking serious questions about our nation's future. Their questions are not inspired by hate, but by concern, concern about a future they don't understand.

The single-minded destruction of Buchanan will send a message to them as well, a message that they must remain silent, that their ideas are not allowed in our national discussion.

No, my grandfather will never vote Republican -- sorry, Pat. But will he bother to vote at all? Why should he, when an entire agenda of issues he cares about are pushed off the table as "fascist?"

What he has seen during this campaign is a demonstration of the unity of purpose of the American "Media-Political Complex," a small but elite group of national figures who will defend at any cost their unchallenged status as rulers of the national conversation. They demand conformity of ideas, subservience of individuality and unquestioning submission to their party philosophy. The unorthodox, like Patrick J. Buchanan, cannot merely be challenged -- they must be destroyed.

That's funny. The Nazis used to do the same thing.

Clinton & Me, Two

January, 1995

Two years ago, the same week William Jefferson Clinton was sworn in as head of our national family, I became a father. One year later, I wrote a column, *Clinton and Me*, in which I noted the frightening similarities in our enthusiastic but inept efforts to execute the duties of our new offices. I ended my article with a lighthearted reference to "the terrible twos."

Ha, ha.

If it helps, Mr. President, there is an American who had an even more bumpy ride in 1994 than you did.

Sure, we got off to a good start. Like the president, I had "The Big Mo" coming into the new year, and I thought 1994 was going to be pretty good. The "Comeback Kid" had health care all but wrapped up in Washington, while my wife and I had reached agreement on a socially progressive budget, with heavy subsidies of such vital programs as the "Tanning Salon Entitlement" and the "Aid to Moms Who Might Eat Their Young if You Don't Get a Sitter Friday Night."

My wife, like yours, Mr. President, took a high-profile role in my administration as well, particularly on the divisive social issue of child discipline. Unfortunately, the resulting plan resembled the HillaryCare scheme in that it worked great until you actually used it. When, for example, my son Mencken discovered his ability to "express himself" through the destruction of property and unorthodox distribution of bodily wastes (we suspect he received NEA funding), my wife and I were completely unprepared.

She suddenly revealed a hidden liberal agenda, fighting my efforts at discipline and adding her maiden name to all family correspondence. Meanwhile, I clung to my more conservative principles and advocated a Singaporean model of social justice: beating the kid's brains in.

19

This division in our leadership left an opening for Mencken who, like the House Republicans, was a master of exploiting weakness. When I discovered him standing over the commode holding the cord of my electric razor (the rest had been roto-rootered), he rushed past me and into the sympathetic arms of his mother. When he sensed she was on the verge of violence, he whipped up a few crocodile tears and clung to my leg. It was transparent political rhetoric, but somehow I couldn't resist.

It was Gerber Gridlock, pure and simple.

Eventually, it became clear that my son considered my commands mere "suggestions," and not particularly worthwhile suggestions at that. If I said, "Put it down," he picked it up. If I said, "Go left," he went right. My administration was rudderless, drifting. My message wasn't penetrating.

Everyone had suggestions as to how we should repair our damaged public image, though we never went as far as you, Mr. President, to invite a psychic and motivational speaker to the White House. I was urged by my father to govern from the Right ("Spare the rod and spoil the child! You got to beat some sense into 'em!") My mother counseled a more liberal approach ("He's just a baby, he didn't mean to hurt anyone. Besides, you can always get another cat...")

Then came the disastrous autumn. Kooks were shooting at the White House, and I was robbed at gunpoint in my driveway. Our poll numbers were plummeting, our wives were on the warpath, and just when it seemed it couldn't get any worse.... Whammo! A chubby-cheeked interloper suddenly stole the limelight and began pushing a radical program of infantile self-promotion.

Newt, meet Alex.

Actually, it's Alexandra. For the second time in less than 20 months, my wife and I had a baby -- the ultimate October surprise.

And talk about dominating the media! Talk about hogging the camera! Like Speaker Gingrich, little Alex can't belch without making headlines. I'm trying to get the family focused on long-term issues (like the need for my wife to be sterilized) and instead the baby-hungry paparazzi spend all day with their heads in the crib, observing every move of my new House leader.

In fact, listening to your pleading tones this past year, Mr. President, I heard a frighteningly familiar sound: the whining voice of a man realizing that no one is paying any attention to what he is saying. Our vocabulary in this second year of parenthood has consisted largely of sighs of frustration and occasional bursts of anger. Meanwhile, no one was listening.

Well, Mr. President, no one said this would be easy. And, in fact, there have been some fun moments.... well, for me, anyway. I have heard it said that being president is the most demanding, frustrating, punishing job in the world, that every president was abused, unappreciated and generally worn plumb out. Yet they all agree that it was the most rewarding part of their careers.

After two years as a father, I know the feeling. Happy birthday, Mencken, and good luck again, Mr. President.

Once again, we're going to need it.

Chapter Two

"The Era Of Big Government Is Over"

Brother Dearest

July, 1996

As Bill Clinton's picayune presidency continues to shrink, his poll numbers expand to nearly gargantuan proportions.

Meanwhile, Americans nostalgic for leadership watch in dismay as President Clinton moves easily from meaningless promises of the impossible ("We shall bring this terrorism to an end!") to breathless pronouncements over the irrelevant (We shall have a new 911 phone system!"). *New York Times* writer Maureen Dowd has dubbed Clinton "President Pothole." She notes with great insight that the President's re-election agenda more closely resembles a run for alderman than leader of the free world.

Listening to the effluvia floating from the White House, one would never know that there are American troops in Bosnia or that our nation's economic expansion is one of the slowest since WWII. What care we if our schools are failing or if the President's drug policy is to get drugs off the streets and into the White House?

But if you're worried about little Johnny watching too much "Mighty Morphin' Power Rangers," President Clinton is on the job.

Clinton and Me

On Monday, President Clinton announced a "landmark" agreement with television broadcasters to air at least three hours a week of educational programs for children. Try to imagine George Washington reaching an agreement with colonial newspapers to print more high-quality cartoons, and the decline of the modern presidency comes clearly into focus.

But this is what big-government liberals do when the era of big government is over. For Bill Clinton, big government is dead, but Big Brother is alive and well.

This is the president who signed into law a measure censoring the Internet so tightly that testimony from lawsuits in which he is personally involved may not be legally transmitted on the Web. This is the president who insists that media moguls stop spreading violence and indecency in the entertainment industry, but who smiles as they spread more than $450,000 into his various campaign coffers.

And this is the president who wants the federal government to regulate the content of commercial television programs to make sure it's "good." Yikes!

Correct me if I'm wrong, but didn't Pat Robertson *lose* his race for the White House?

The theory of big "L" liberalism (the Clintons' brand) is that people ought to be good and, if they won't, the government should make them. So, if those bad ol' TV networks don't put enough educational programs on the air, the government will force them to do it by threatening to take away their licenses.

There, that was easy. Now, what about those publishers who don't print enough "Clinton-friendly" novels...

President Clinton and the Niceness Nazis would have a point if the problem were the lack of "good" shows. But in fact there are just as many quality kids' shows as kids will stand, and that ain't many.

Mandating three hours a week of "good" children's television (when you figure out what *that* is, please call the FCC) only solves the picayune problem of broadcasting government-approved programs. Getting young citizens to sit still and watch them is the real trick.

We already have a government-run TV network with 24 hours of official, government-sanctioned programming every day. Much of it is for children, real quality stuff like "Barney" and "Teletubbies."

What's worse is that the problem of trashy TV and decline of family fare is one the market has already solved: New family-friendly TV networks are springing up on cable, the satellite dish, the Internet and everywhere else. TV networks love bragging about "family hour" and the unwatchable, whitewashed drivel they are producing for it.

Just a note to the Clintons: The secret to programming TV isn't ranting -- it's *ratings.*

The general reaction of the general public to such generally annoying initiatives like the President's is usually a shrug: "So, it won't make kids' TV any better, so what? What harm can it do?"

And if you don't count little things like poking a hole in the First Amendment or destroying the liberty of a few individual TV station owners, you're right. The costs are small, the effects negligible.

Just about the right size, in fact, for an incredible shrinking president.

Guru To You, Too

June, 1996

"Caricatured as Hillary's New Age Svengali, Jean Houston offers myths and mantras that may seem strange, but are right in the baby-boom mainstream"-- Newsweek.

There was a moment during the Filegate hearings -- when the head of security in the White House personnel office announced that he had never actually been *hired* -- that I looked up from the TV set and thought: "Yes, there is a God."

In these heady days, with Clinton apparatchiks waking each morning intent upon humiliating themselves on national television, it is tempting to believe that a divine hand is guiding their ill fortune. Indeed, it's hard to believe that mere mortals are capable of this level of incompetence without help from the Great Beyond.

Alas, I am an infidel and must lay the daily sins of stupidity at the feet of Mr. and Mrs. Clinton. Watching these two obviously intelligent and politically savvy operators immolate in their own hubris is not a pleasant sight, even for a right-wing wacko like me. I would like to believe there is some divine purpose to their incompetence, but I cannot in good conscience blame God for the Clinton White House.

He didn't vote for them -- *we* did.

Instead of thinking of the Presidential Buffoons as God's punishment, I think of them as the natural result of democracy. Looking around at America, it seems we have precisely the First Family that we deserve.

The Clintons live in the paradoxes that plague the American character: They are simultaneously ethically flaccid and morally rigid, finding easy ways to work around their own ethics while stridently demanding good, clean livin' from the rest of us.

The Clintons are also wildly ambitious, yet unrelenting in their pursuit of public policies to punish those who achieve. And the most annoying paradox to me personally, Bill and Hillary Clinton are both thoroughly secular and untiringly religious.

For a couple of world-weary baby boomers, President and Mrs. Clinton have a breath takingly metaphysical naiveté: They'll believe in just about anything -- even themselves.

It's been interesting to watch the GLUMs (Godless Liberal Media-types) cover the story of "Hillary's Rasputin," Dr. Jean Houston. Reporters who have never had a kind word for any religious sensibilities trumpet Mrs. Clinton's "deeply held Methodist faith" -- demonstrating at once their willingness to suck up to the First Lady, and their complete lack of knowledge concerning modern-day Methodism.

A Methodist service inspires all the religious fervor of a Rotary Club luncheon -- the only difference being the Rotarians occasionally read from the Bible. A devout Methodist is almost as hard to imagine as a Quaker terrorist.

At the same time, the press has gone to great lengths to note that Mrs. Clinton's meetings with the self-declared "doctor," (she reportedly lied on her resume about having a doctorate from Columbia University) were not séances or spiritualism. "Dr." Houston is not a psychic, but rather a "sacred psychologist," we are told pointedly.

The conclusion being that, while Mrs. Clinton is devoutly religious and imbued with the sacred, it's not like she actually believes in God.

In America, the land of Sally Jesse and TV psychics, this all makes perfect sense. Why condemn Hillary Clinton for doing the White House equivalent of calling Dionne Warwick's Psychic Friends Network?

And I agree. Mrs. Clinton is no more stupid for hanging out with "Jean Houston -- Sacred Psychologist" than you and I are for getting a reading from "Madame Zelda -- Psychic Chiropractor."

Perhaps you think it's unfair to compare Houston to a spiritualist when she says she doesn't do séances. Once again, I agree. Indeed, this is the most disturbing part of Mrs. Clinton's "journey of faith." There is none.

If Mrs. Clinton were having truly spiritual experiences -- achieving Nirvana, speaking in tongues, running a backhoe over the cast of "Friends" -- there would be some faithfulness on her part to respect. But there is no spirit in Mrs. Clinton's spirituality.

For old-time Methodists, "seeking God" meant going to church and praying to the Risen Lord; for Hillary Clinton, it means hiring a sacred psychologist and talking to Eleanor Roosevelt.

This sort of faux-religious experimentation is the metaphysical version of "I didn't inhale." It is typical of people who feel they ought to believe in something because believing in something is nice, but they don't want to be, you know, *weird* about it. In the end, they have just enough non-rational tenets to believe that you should stop sinning, but not enough faith to believe that they should, too.

In other words, they are hypocrites. The result of this sort of "religion without faith" is always hypocrisy. Thus, we have a White House that can support partial birth abortions but violently attacks tobacco, an administration that thinks nothing of poking through your FBI file but maintains its position as the first ever to refuse to release the President's medical files.

So whether it's Dr. Jean Houston, Mr. Tony Robbins or the Rev. Al Sharpton, the news from the White House this week is much the same as last: It is a place where anything can happen...if you're willing to believe in anything.

Keyed Up

March, 1996

I'm no James Carville, but it seems to me that two things a candidate for president never wants to do are:

a) Go on a hunger strike.

b) Get detained by the police.

Alan Keyes has done both in the same week.

Last Sunday, police officers had to forcibly remove Mr. Keyes from an Atlanta TV station that was hosting a presidential debate to which he was not invited. "As Martin Luther King went to jail in order to secure my right to participate, I go to jail in order to exercise that right," Keyes bellowed as he was led away. "My only crie is that I am qualified to be president!"

Three days earlier, Keyes launched a hunger strike to protest his exclusion from a debate in Columbia, S.C. "I shall take in neither food nor drink," he intoned biblically, "until my ideas and my campaign are taken seriously."

I'm afraid Mr. Keyes is going to get very hungry.

While the voters have declined to take his campaign seriously, Alan Keyes continues to liven up the 1996 presidential race. He has an amazing effect on Republican audiences, particularly down South. Mixing a conservative, anti-government diatribe with a heavy dose of brimstone, Alan Keyes is the perfect speaker for any group of guilty, white Republicans (how redundant is *that?*) in need of a good spanking.

He preaches that America is a spiritual wasteland, we're all going to hell in a hand basket, and abortion is the great moral crisis of our day...though not so great as to cause Mr. Keyes to skip a meal over it.

Indeed, as far as I can discover, Alan Keyes has never gone hungry, been jailed or received so much as a jaywalking ticket in his tireless fight against abortion.

So much for great moral crises...

But there is a bigger issue raised by the embarrassingly goofy candidacy of Alan Keyes and the serious treatment he's receiving from the media. The fact is, Alan Keyes is getting away with this nonsense because he is black.

The Keyes candidacy is yet another example of the media's condescending attitude toward black people. Accepted norms of behavior and the otherwise sacrosanct rules of journalism are all cast overboard in the presence of any prominent, yet stupid, person who happens to be black.

For example, Mr. Keyes wasn't the only presidential candidate excluded from recent debates. Established political figures seeking the presidency, such as Sen. Richard Lugar (R.-Insomnia) were also left out of the same events -- but without hunger strikes or hissy fits. They may not be happy, but they're behaving.

Now, try to imagine the media reaction if "B-1" Bob Dornan (R.-Rush Limbaugh's Lap) had been arrested at a debate site and started invoking the name of Martin Luther King. The comedy of it alone would make the story big news, maybe front page. But for Alan Keyes? Buried with the obits.

Keyes' behavior is shameful and juvenile. He should be publicly mocked at every turn. Instead, interviewers nod compassionately while he spouts more incoherent gibberish. He's being held to a different standard because wimpy, liberal types -- in their heart of hearts -- don't believe black people are capable of measuring up to reasonable standards of behavior.

An even more glaring example is Louis Farrakhan who, even if he dropped the "dirty Jews" talk, would still be one of the most moronic national figures of our day. I was particularly impressed when he went to Nigeria to urge the citizenry to be more supportive of the brutal military dictatorship currently oppressing them.

Try to imagine a white politician touring South Africa to support Apartheid or an Hispanic-American cruising Chile with Pinochet. They would be universally denounced. But Minister Farrakhan is given a bye. "He doesn't know any better," nervous editorialists tut-tut. "It's a black thing, you wouldn't understand."

No. It's a stupid thing. I *do* understand. Stupidity knows no racial or ethnic bounds. Rich or poor, black or white, straight or gay--stupid can afflict us all. Pretending that dumb actions by black people are reasonable isn't compassion; it's racism of a most pernicious sort.

One last note on the media and race: A friend of mine got into trouble a few years ago when he hired an unemployed, black fisherman to run in a Republican primary election. It was a cynical ploy to increase white turnout, and it didn't work.

But what did work was the media condescension factor. The "candidate," who was not even registered to vote when he entered the race, could barely read and write and was utterly unfamiliar with the office he had been hired to seek. However, a reporter tracked him down and interviewed him -- no mean feat given the gentleman's lack of grammar and limited vocabulary.

But instead of an expose' of a clearly incompetent candidate, the reporter repaired the grammar, developed some sentence fragments into policy statements and cranked out a 30-inch story that dressed up this bozo like a statesman. Fortunately for the democratic process, nobody read the article and the candidate lost.

Somewhere there's a voter trying to make an honest judgment about the candidates who has no idea how loony Alan Keyes is because no one will tell him. If he knew, he would never give the candidate his vote.

A sandwich, maybe...

B.M.O.C.

May, 1996

Jermaine O'Neal is a South Carolina basketball phenom, a born superstar who combines the two attributes vital to success in professional sports: overactive glands and underachieving intellect. After spending four years mopping the floor with his high school counterparts, Jermaine made headlines when he decided to skip college and head straight to the NBA--and the accompanying multi-million dollar contracts.

The young man's decision sparked heated debate, around the NBA and at local cocktail parties, over the question of whether or not it is good/wise/moral for a young man like Mr. O'Neal to miss the tremendous opportunities offered by America's institutions of higher learning. Can mere money compare to the exquisite experience of undergraduate life in the halls of academe?

As a successful college graduate and former master's candidate, I can answer with complete confidence:

"Jermaine! TAKE THE CASH!"

I make this suggestion with no thought of O'Neal's ability to succeed in the pros. I have no idea and even less interest. If someone wants to pay this adenoidally advanced young man a billion dollars to sit on the bench and wear inflatable sneakers, I say, "Congratulations!"

What does rattle my cage is the underlying notion about college that drives this argument. "There is something wrong," reads the *San Jose Mercury News*, "when young men decide against an all-expenses' paid college education for the chance to grab the wealth and stardom of pro basketball."

"Tut, tut," cluck the callers on local talk radio. "How can this poor young man be allowed to set aside his education to pursue a quick buck? Shame, shame!"

How about "yank, yank?"

The premise put forward by the do-gooders is that everyone who can go to college, should. They are wrong on two points:

a) No, they shouldn't.

b) He can't.

O'Neal's leapfrog over the NCAA and onto the big-league hardwoods was not inspired by ambition but by ineptitude. He would like to play a year or two in the NBA minor-league system (read: college basketball) but can't get into a "real school," i.e., one without the word "Technical" in its name. O'Neal just doesn't have the grades.

To be eligible for a Division I school, O'Neal would have to add 100 points to his best SAT score of 830 -- an unlikely event for a young man who missed his last SAT exam because *he couldn't find the right building!*

ATTN: Harvard! Do you have this guy's home phone number?

I don't mean to pick on O'Neal, really, I don't. I feel sorry for him because he is hitting his head against America's wall of hypocrisy on higher education. If O'Neal were a carpenter, a cook or a chiropractor, he would be welcome to practice his profession without spending more than an afternoon in his local library.

But because he is an athlete, he must endure four years of crib sheets and curved grades to prove he is worthy of his profession. He is required to waste four years of his economic life on a pursuit he has already demonstrated he has no interest in whatsoever -- his brain.

This is not necessarily a bad thing. Not everyone has the interest or ability for astronomy or calculus. Not everyone belongs in college at all. Indeed, America was built by men and women who had nothing more than a moderate education, but were blessed with good sense and willingness to work.

The result of encouraging unwilling or incompetent students into our colleges is easy to measure. Sit down this week with one of our freshly minted college grads and after an hour of conversation, try and figure out what he or she actually got for that $40,000 in tuition...besides a future of dodging phone calls from the Student Loan Nazis.

The real question, the obvious question, is never asked, namely, "What are all these people doing in college in the first place?" The fact is, half of today's students are as out of place in college as Michael Jackson at a school for wayward boys.

As a former grad student at a certain public university in Columbia, S.C. (no names, but its initials are U.S.C.), I spent time, up close, with the pride of the Confederacy. While some students are intelligent, motivated and determined to get an education, many simply have no idea what the purpose of their college career is...except that it somehow involves the keg in their dorm.

I once met a student in her early twenties who had $50,000 in student loans and was still years away from getting her degree. Her major was Holistic Anthropology with a minor in Tarot Cards or some such blather, so her economic outlook was exceedingly dim. Had she borrowed the 50 grand and built a house, she would at least be unemployed with a roof over her head. Instead, it's as though she dropped a wad in Vegas and hopes to find a job for a "people person" at 25k per annum before Guido gets her home address.

She never belonged in college, and neither does Jermaine O'Neal. Indeed, there are only three legitimate reasons to spend major bucks for college: to get a job, to get married or to get an education. In that order.

For certain fields -- biology, engineering, political correctness stormtrooping -- college is essentially a tech school. For such students, the only difference between a university and Clyde's School of Chiropractic and Auto-Diesel Mechanics is that Clyde doesn't force you to waste time in courses like "New Age Elizabethan Poetry" or "Erotic Photography as Rococo Art."

As for marriage, this may be the single most useful service to society performed by institutions of higher education. Thanks to extremely "liberal" admissions standards at most universities ("Can you spell 'SAT?' You're in!"), the gene pool is tremendously mixed. Plumbers' sons and bank presidents' daughters are flung together with abandon, often at a period in life when their hormones are taking no prisoners. This is one reason why class envy has never taken hold in America. Junior may not have the brains to achieve greatness, but thanks to our national coeducational policy, he can marry it.

People who claim they are in college just to "get a good education" are always lying. Run into a philosophy major at a kegger and you'll hear: "Just getting an education makes me a better person, more well-rounded, more competitive. I'm really proud of my degree in Transactional Sumerian Psychology -- say, doesn't your dad work at the Highway Department? Think he could get me in?"

Meanwhile, the students who are seriously committed to learning something -- clearly a minority -- are shafted by the current "lowest common denominator" system. Classes move slowly while the professor tries to explain to basketball players and bimbettes that cosines aren't what your dad gives the bank so you can get a lower car payment.

In the early 1990s I found myself, through a circumstance too painful to recall, trapped in 100-level philosophy class. On our first exam, with a modicum of preparation, several classmates and I scored a 95. After the curve was applied, we discovered that a 35 was a "B" and an 18 was a "C." More amazing was the idiot sitting in front of me who complained that the class was too hard. His test score: an 8.

You say that's typical undergraduate work, that grad school is different? Then come meet the Doctor of Education candidate who has a Master's from NYU and cannot read. In her thirties and with kids, when I met her, she hadn't worked in years -- though she said she was certified to teach (not English, I prayed, after listening to her bludgeon the language into submission). She literally could not read her financial aid form or answer simple questions like "What year did you graduate?" Yet, here she was, waiting for another $12,000 in taxpayer payoffs. And she got it.

The cost of education is spiraling ever upward for one reason: demand. Too many people -- make that "stupid people"--are going to college when they should be going to a trade school, apprentice programs or into multi-level marketing. The only way to get these students through the most meager courses is grade inflation, which means the value of every degree declines, which means you need another degree to indicate academic excellence, which means more people going to grad school, which means more doctorates, etc., etc.

The solution? Stop sending the Jermaine O'Neals of the world to college, and make it tougher, not easier, for everyone else.

President Clinton's *"tax increase/deficit reduction/budget balancing/the deficit still goes up a trillion bucks/ha ha"* plan included a federal Direct Lending program, which will make it easier for young people to take out loans they can't afford to take classes they don't want for a degree they can't use.

Now that's what I call compassion.

If you think I'm being too rough on college students, sit down and talk with a few. After your headache goes away, write me and apologize. If you don't know how to write, call your local financial aid office and tell them you're an education major at an American university. Your check is in the mail.

Olympics Of The Damned

July, 1996

As the mystery surrounding the crash of TWA Flight 800 continues, one nagging question comes to my mind again and again: Where was Stone Philips when the plane went down?

My suspicions drift towards Stone, not because he has the second-dumbest name in contemporary broadcasting (Wolf Blitzer still holds a commanding lead), but because he works for *Dateline NBC*. *Dateline* has two strikes against it: First, they have a penchant for blowing things up to create news (just ask General Motors) and second, it's on NBC -- also known as the "Nightly Body Count" network.

NBC is absolutely obsessed with death. This realization came to me as I was watching their coverage of the 1996 Olympics in Atlanta which, as of press time, features more dead people per frame then a driver's ed training film.

It must be some Clinton administration mandate for the media to feel people's pain. Virtually every event, seemingly every athlete, is profiled by NBC in context of a related death, some of them recent and some not: Swimmers who just lost a parent, a Greco-Roman wrestler whose brother died in a car accident. For the producers at NBC Sports, the most competitive events aren't track and field or gymnastics, but Olympic bucket kicking and 100-meter freestyle grave digging.

If you've watched even a few token minutes of the "Coca-Cola 100" (as the Games are known in Atlanta), you must know what I'm talking about. The cameras are live at the track or in the arena, the athletes are waiting for the gun, then suddenly, the theme to *Love Story* begins, and we segue to a pre-taped shot of an Olympian walking pensively along a lonely road.

"When she goes for the gold later today, Suzy Shaumberg of Oakbrook, Illinois, won't just be shooting at clay pigeons," Bob Costas intones in a funereal hush, " she'll also be firing rounds of remorse from a tragic air rifle accident that claimed the life of her half-sister, Molly, just three years ago."

Then comes the close-up of the brave, teary-eyed athlete talking about her loved one, as home footage of the deceased is superimposed across the screen.

Apparently, for NBC the tension of a teen-ager doing backflips on a high beam before a television audience of 1 billion people isn't quite enough. They need pathos. They need anguish.

They need a corpse.

The TWA tragedy gave us 200 of them just weeks before the Olympics, and NBC is determined to work each one into a special report. Every tenuous connection between the human horror in Long Island and the media horror show in Atlanta is highlighted, pulled to the breaking point:

"Here we are with Olympic diver John McDougal ... John, are you haunted by the fact that you yourself once flew on a 747 early in your training?"

Sports reporters hang like ectoplasm on the lives of these athletes who have already faced almost unimaginable trials just to get to the Olympics. Most of these kids have trained for years -- even decades -- competed in round after round of qualifiers at the local, state and national levels. Their participation in the Games is proof that these young athletes can do something that is very hard, very well, over and over again.

They get to the Olympics ... only to be besieged by mic-waving media morticians pushing them to "release their pain" about some personal tragedy -- real or imagined. I keep waiting for one of the athletes to just explode. It would have to be an American because the other athletes (with the possible exception of the French) are too polite.

And the other nations' athletes are largely spared this experience because they're foreigners and who cares if they die, anyway? (Once again with the possible exception of the French.)

I pray that before the Olympics are over, some high-strung athlete will turn to an NBC reporter and say: "Shut up! Just SHUT UP! Yes, my coach's manicurist died last Thursday on the way to the Games! And yes, no American has won a medal in this event without a manicured coach in a non-boycotted Olympics since the Berlin games of 1936, and yes, I'm a little worried right now. Wouldn't *you* be a little nervous if two-thirds of the world's population were watching you dive 75 feet into crystal clear water wearing nothing but a Speedo on live television? Now get off my back, you mic-waving moron before I shove Willard's hairpiece up your---!"

In their melodramatic attempts to humanize the already painfully human stories of the Olympics, NBC is only succeeding in marginalizing these stories. Just as films such as *Independence Day* lose all the emotive power of death by killing virtually everyone, the non-stop pseudo-tragedies of overblown media coverage destroy the power of the true human dramas it touches.

It is a destruction far more tragic than the events themselves -- the death of our sensibility towards death. Stone Philips and a busload of dynamite couldn't do as much damage, not even in prime time.

Jesse Goes To Hollywood

March, 1996

``Where we're coming from, we totally understand the dire needs of commercial cinema. We know that until the audiences walk into the theater, you're really nobody." -- India's leading movie director Shekhar Kapur, explaining the success of Asian directors in Hollywood.*

I don't know what the current rate of unemployment is for black males, but it is too high by one. Someone has *got* to find a job for Jesse Jackson.

Idle hands are the devil's playground, and when there isn't a Democratic presidential primary to grandstand or restaurant chain to shake down, the Reverend Jackson falls prey to mischievous demons. He starts seeing things: a reasonable side to Louis Farrakhan, an efficient city government in Washington, D.C. and a racist regime at Hollywood and Vine.

Yes, Hollywood is a stronghold of the Aryan Nations and the Klan, says Jackson, because not enough Academy Award nominees are black. Then again, quite a few nominees are Jewish, but, hey, maybe the Hollywood Klan is more progressive then their branch offices in the rural South. Anyway, Jackson knows racism (and a mega-media opportunity) when he sees it, and the Right Reverend is going to get Tinseltown to see the light.

His Oscar-night effort, entitled "Lights, Camera, Affirmative Action," (ouch!) involved an unenthusiastic handful of marchers gathered around Jackson outside the Hollywood studios of KABC, the Los Angeles affiliate broadcasting the Oscars. Jackson was, as usual, simultaneously articulate and over-reaching: "(There is) racial exclusion, cultural distortion, lack of employment opportunities, lack of positions of authority.... It doesn't stand to reason that if you are forced to the back of the bus, you will go to the bus company's annual picnic and act like you're happy," Jackson said.

His supporters were even more direct, carrying placards saying "Same slavemaster, different plantation."

Well, excuse me if I'm not ready to declare war on southern California and march on the Dorothy Chandler Pavilion. Maybe it's because I'm from South Carolina and get to see real-live racism up close and personal, the kind of racism that gets black college students dragged out of their cars and beaten by overzealous highway patrolmen.

Or maybe it's because I spent Oscar night listening to Whoopie Goldberg's monologue, Quincy Jones' music, Oprah Winfrey's shameless sucking up and Will Smith stumbling over his lines.

Or maybe, just maybe, the tired cry of racism has come so many times from the self-appointed shepherds of black America that even liberals and journalists are beginning to have second thoughts.

In choosing Hollywood as his target, Jesse Jackson has done more than just alienate his base (i.e., guilty white people with more money then brains). He has chosen the one field in which affirmative action, aka "quotas," will never be effective -- the entertainment industry.

No amount of civil rights legislation could force people to sit through Eddie Murphy's *Vampire in Brooklyn*, and no amount of secret racist plotting by the ADL and the John Birchers could keep Americans from flocking to *Beverly Hills Cop*. (It took two sequels to do that.)

The entertainment industry is the ultimate merit-pay system. How much you are worth is directly proportional to how much people will pay to see you. No quotas, no weighted admissions system, no "excellence through diversity." Whoever puts the most butts in the most seats wins. Period.

Quotas don't work in industries where individual performance matters. Jackson's race-based bean counting is better suited for fields where mediocrity is a career advantage.

Thus, Jackson and his gang have had great success in the bureaucracies of academia and corporate America, where losers of all races are easy to hide. But where do you hide an underachiever on a basketball team or a tennis court? Where do you hide your unqualified quota hires on a Broadway stage?

I will concede to the Reverend Jackson (and anyone else) that the Academy Awards themselves are not merit based. They are, largely, a joke. This year's debacle -- no "best picture" nominations for *Nixon* or *12 Monkeys* but one for a pig movie -- is typical for the intellectual lightweights who are members of the so-called "Academy."

But the Academy Awards aren't a joke because of racism; they're a joke because of the pedestrian mores of the Academy members themselves.

Whoopie Goldberg's Oscar, for example, came *not* from her starring role in *The Color Purple* but from her phoned-in performance in a cheesy romance called *Ghost*. It was, however, a cheesy romance that made a whole lot of money, and that's how to get the Academy's attention.

But if Jackson manages to convince the "Academics" who hand out the Oscars to set aside a certain number of nominations for minority actors, more power to him. Indeed, in a spirit of cooperation, I would like to make the first nomination in such a special category, Best Black Actor of 1995: O.J. Simpson.

And Jesse Jackson thinks black actors can't get a break in LA.

A Southern Man

October, 1996

"This is a tragic day for America when Negro agitators, spurred on by communist enticements to promote racial strife, can cause the United States Senate to be steamrollered into passing the worst, most unreasonable and unconstitutional legislation that has ever been considered by the Congress."-- Strom Thurmond, on passage of the 1964 Civil Rights Act.

On a recent trip to Chicago, a friend was driving me past a cemetery on the North Side, and I noticed the top of the walls was lined with barbed wire.

"Let me guess," I told him with a laugh. "You only do that on election years. Slowing them down on their way to the polls, right?"

My friend, a proud native of America's most corrupt political city, responded angrily: "What? Are you saying no dead people ever vote in South Carolina?"

"Are you kidding?" I shot back. "Dead people don't vote in our elections -- they *run* in them! Hell, they even *win!*"

And so the laughable corruption of Chicago and the hilarious stupidity of South Carolina converged for a brief, shining moment in this otherwise humorless election year. With the presidential race turning into a blowout of Atlanta Brave-esque proportions, the pathetic farce of the eighth Strom Thurmond U.S. Senate campaign is a much-needed seventh-inning stretch.

"All the laws of Washington and all the bayonets of the Army cannot force the Negro into our homes, our schools, our churches and places of recreation."--Strom Thurmond, 1948.

Like all farces, the ending is both outrageous and predictable. That Strom Thurmond is going to be re-elected in a landslide goes without saying. In any election, particularly in South Carolina, one of the most dependable predictors of Election Day behavior is to ask yourself: "Is there any candidate for public office who is so incompetent or embarrassing that to vote for him would require a overwhelming display of ignorance or stupidity?" When you've found such a candidate, bet the farm. You've got yourself a sure winner.

Such a candidate is Strom Thurmond. It's hard to imagine a more unpleasant convergence of gross personal incompetence and vile political philosophy. Most political consultants would kill to run against either a 94-year-old drooler who can't stay awake through a committee hearing or an icon of racism who filibustered for 24 hours to keep "darkies" out of public restaurants. In a race against Strom Thurmond -- you get *both!*

And yet, Strom Thurmond's opponents -- in the primary and general elections -- have made little headway against the Great Methuselah. Why?

Because most political campaigns are arguments about what is best for you, the voter. "Elect me," the candidates claim, "and I will make you richer, happier, stronger, faster." There is no such argument for voting for Strom Thurmond. It is impossible for the Thurmond camp to argue that their candidate is going to do anything about crime or taxes or teen-age pregnancy (well, actually...) because it is impossible to argue he is going to do anything at all.

They're left with campaign slogans like: "Strom Thurmond: Getting Out Of Bed For Over 94% of a Century!" Or "Strom: He'll PROBABLY Show Up!"

"I have done more for black people than any other person in the nation, North or South."

Indeed, the notion that Strom Thurmond is a senator is purely delusional, a delusion the good Senator clings to desperately. He is no more familiar with the force structure of the Armed Services (whose Senate committee he chairs) then he is with the lyrics of the Macarena.

Despite these truths, the Senator is a lock on Election Day. Another reason for his certain success is that the people covering this race are giving Senator Thurmond a "bye." No one takes him seriously as a senator. When opponents point out his poor record protecting South Carolina jobs (we lost more jobs to military base closings than any state in the Union), reporters simply yawn. "Of course he's incompetent: He's 93 years old!" When opponents run TV ads pointing out that he's too old, reporters write: "Desperate challengers make issue of Thurmond's age, ignore substance!"

It's the ultimate political strategy: presumed incompetence. And it works.

Much has been made, by the way, of TV ads (one of which I wrote) talking about Thurmond's age. Polling seems to indicate that viewers of all ages react violently against them. Pundits say this backlash is an indicator that South Carolinians think making age an issue is unfair.

In fact, this is backwards. Targeting Thurmond's obvious physical inability is *too* fair. As Mencken noted, "Any man can bear injustice. What stings is justice." The voters of South Carolina are going to vote for Thurmond, they know it is obviously foolish and indefensible, and the more clearly you point out the obvious, the angrier they get.

"Hooray for Strom Thurmond.... Southern men stand up for themselves, for their friends and for their families. And Thurmond's a southern man." -- South Carolina GOP Chairman Henry McMaster after Thurmond shoved a USAir flight attendant.

Like the drunkard stumbling toward his waiting car or the secretary pulling into the parking space outside her married boss's motel room, the last thing these people want to hear is reason. They're going to vote for Thurmond, even if they have to follow him to the graveyard to do it.

One day -- and I sincerely hope it is in the distant future -- J. Strom Thurmond will finally succumb to his own mortality. I trust he will be remembered for the whole man: his racism, his heroism, his selfless commitment to public service, his selfish refusal to relinquish the political spotlight. But if Senator Thurmond were to honestly write his own epitaph, I believe his gravestone would read: "Jes' One Mo' Term!"

My other prediction: He would win in a landslide.

Chapter 3

"The Most Ethical Administration In American History"

Just Say No

August, 1996

"I never vote for anyone. I always vote against."--W. C. Fields

President Bill Clinton, the Houdini of American politics, has done the impossible: He's gotten me excited about voting for Bob Dole.

I have never, ever voted for Bob Dole. Not in '88, not this year, not ever. It has been a point of personal pride, for Bob Dole is one of the most repulsive Republicans in contemporary America. He brings together the grand political vision of George Bush and the warmth of human spirit of Richard Nixon. He is, in short, everything I revile about Republican politics.

But I will vote for him on November 5, and I will do so with pride. Which is a statement that cannot be made by *any* American voting to re-elect President Clinton, a candidate whose supporters can only feel shame.

Now, shame is not necessarily a sufficient reason to change your vote. I voted for George Bush in 1992, and I was very ashamed to do so at the time. But I was willing to acknowledge my shame, to acknowledge that President Bush had done nothing to earn my (or any other rational conservative's) vote.

But, while I wasn't too thrilled about voting for the worst Republican president since William Howard Taft, it is beyond my ability to imagine myself voting for the worst president since George Bush: William Jefferson Clinton.

President Clinton is, quite simply, a man without shame. There is no lie so obvious, no posturing so political, no insincere emotional display so nauseating that he will refrain from throwing his entire 250 pounds of self-righteous egomania into it. There are no limits to his self-deception, no borders to his buffoonery. And in the long litany of scams, shams and flimflams being run out of the White House these days, none demonstrates so clearly the shamelessness of the Clintons than "Filegate."

Filegate began when the Clinton administration put longtime Democrat hack Craig Livingstone in charge of White House personnel security...despite the fact that his only prior "security" experience involved Hillary-watch duty outside a gently rocking state patrol car in a Little Rock parking lot.

Livingstone, unsurprisingly, chose another Democratic hanger-on, Anthony Marceca, as his assistant. Their job was to review the security status of people who would be regularly roaming the Clinton White House. In doing so, they requested the personal FBI files of an untold number (around 800 or so) of American citizens -- all *Republicans*. ("Here's a White House request for the file on Reagan, Ronald W. Hmmmm.... I wonder what cabinet post he's up for...")

Why this sudden surge of bipartisanship in the Clinton White House? And how were these political hacks able to get these sensitive files using nothing more than unsigned form letters?

Now, unsigned requests for secret FBI documents would normally be ignored...at least, I hope so. If not, then you and I could send over a blind request for Elvis's files and wrap up this whole JFK/Jimmy Hoffa thing in a weekend. So why then would the FBI even honor these anonymous file requests from the Clintons in the first place?

Because another Clinton political hack, Louis Freeh, is in charge of the FBI. Boing!

If that were the end of it -- a president violates the privacy rights of hundreds of political opponents in an apparent attempt to gain political advantage -- I would just laugh it off as the usual political sleaze. But the President will have none of that. His policy is to deny, not only that anyone in his White House has done any wrong, but that it is unimaginable that the morally superior inhabitants of 1600 Pennsylvania Avenue would possibly do anything so, so, (oooh) political.

So, when the President's spokesman was first asked if Livingstone was a political operative, the answer was no. The next day, the answer was yes, but only after about a million newspapers reported that Livingstone had worked on numerous campaigns, including President Clinton's.

Then, when Republicans began to suggest that a political operative might want political files for political reasons (another wild GOP conspiracy theory), the White House attorney said no, because "my own investigation of the files controversy found there is nothing to indicate that there is a political motivation behind this."

Now *that's* assuring...

But the final insult to us all was when the Clinton administration tried to blame the mess on previous presidents. The Clinton stooges argued that FBI files have been obtained this way for 30 years, and any other president could have done the same thing.

Which is the perfect time to note that they didn't. No other president -- not Reagan when the Democrats had the Congress, not LBJ when Vietnam was red hot, not Carter when he was about to get his electoral brains beaten in -- no president was willing to use the federal police force as his personal private eye for potential political dirt.

There is something these other presidents have that President Clinton does not: shame. They may not have had much, but for presidents as revered as Kennedy and as reviled as Nixon, there was a line out there somewhere they would not cross: a deed too foul, a demand too great, some something they wouldn't do to be re-elected.

We cannot honestly count Bill Clinton among these men.

Meanwhile, there are a lot of things Bob Dole won't do to get elected (like figure out why he wants to be president). And that is the reason he's got my vote.

To Di For

September, 1997

"...the basic game of photographer and quarry will not essentially change...the stars want the media, when they want them. That won't stop."--Chris Steele-Perkins, Parisian photography agent.

The day after The Wreck, I was asked by a reporter if I knew Prince Charles' last name. "Stuart?" I guessed. "Something royal. I don't know...Tudor? Windsor? Montague? Capulet?" Such is my ignorance on all matters royal.

I am told the royal wedding that gave the world Prince Charles and Princess Diana was viewed by three-quarters of a billion people in 76 countries, but I must have been watching *Jeopardy* at the time. Indeed, a Botswanan sheep-herder could clean my game-show clock if Alex Trebek called out "Lifestyles of the British Monarchy for $500!"

A week ago, everything I knew about the Royals could fit on the back of Dan Quayle's resume. Today, I know more about Lady Di than I do about my own mother, whether I like it or not.

I cannot recall the last media feeding frenzy as all-consuming as the death of Her Divorceship. I was headed from New York to Philly the night of the wreck, spinning through the radio dial looking for traffic and weather reports. Forget it. My dashboard had become "All Di, All the Time! -- We've Got Di Dead on the 8's: 18, 28, 38, 48 and 58 After the Hour! Give Us 22 Minutes, and We'll Give You The Princess...Dead!"

My local paper was even worse. The daily comes out with four sections: world news, local news, sports and the wimpy "lifestyle/arts" section. The Monday after Di's death -- I swear this is true -- my local yokel "Di wouldn't come to this town on a bet" newspaper had nothing but Di on the front page of three of the four sections: nothing else! Not

51

a single non-Di story anywhere on the front except in the sports section, where Di was relegated to page 3.

Why? What am I missing? I'm sorry, folks, but your fascination with the royal family completely escapes me. And I am particularly bewildered by your irrational connection to the white-trash wonder of the world, Lady Di.

Every news story is filled with quotes from maudlin members of the Great Unwashed, weeping for "the People's Princess" (a notion as internally consistent as "the Beloved Despot.") "It's like we've lost one of our own political figures," said Joni Van Vliet, 18, of Bend, Oregon, proving in one fell swoop that

a) The Oregon public school system is a disaster

b) American newspapers will print *anything.*

And I mean anything. Newsrooms across America, desperate to localize Di's death, had their reporters scouring the streets for anything remotely related to the British Isles. Ordering an English muffin at a sidewalk cafe could get you five minutes on the local news. My favorite was the news radio station whose reporter made a mad dash Sunday morning to the local Anglican Church. ("Hey, aren't they the Church of *England*? Grab your mic and let's roll!")

And it worked. In such Anglophilic enclaves as Germantown, Pa., and Fond-du-Lac, Wi., the locals choked, sighed and sobbed on cue over the shocking death of this beautiful and tragic hero who meant so much to us all.

Watching Americans react to the media coverage of Princess Di's death is a lot like watching the audience in the Tony and Tina's Wedding plays that are all the rage off-Broadway. In these plays, the audience members are supposed to be family members attending the wedding or bar mitzvah or whatever, and they are expected to interact with the professionals in the show.

So too with the average citizen when the TV camera comes on: People know they are supposed to be upset because, well, everyone else seems upset, so why not just play along?

If the newspapers say Lady Di's a tragic figure, then she's a tragic figure -- though the tragedy of a life that began in aristocracy, blossomed at Buckingham Palace and ended in the back seat of a millionaire's Mercedes escapes me.

Clearly, Diana's death is a tragedy -- every death is. But how can anyone use the word tragedy to describe Diana's life?

She got divorced, sure. So do 50 percent of all married Americans, but how many of them get out with $26.5 million in cash and $600,000 a year in walking-around money?

Yes, Lady Di had bulimia and was depressed -- but why? Because her husband was doinking around? That's the sad tale of every country/western song on the jukebox and, besides, so was she. One reason "royal watchers" were enthusiastic about her relationship with Dodi was that Di was finally dating somebody single.

Sure, Diana had an overbearing mother-in-law and her every haircut was on the cover of a tabloid, but if a life of Swiss finishing schools, fantastic wealth and a castle filled with servants is "tragic," then I say: "Hey, Alex! I'll take "Tragedy" for $27 million!"

But pointing out these obvious facts is not part of the game, the game that the tabloids, their mainstream press allies and the millions of mall-coifed females who finance them want to play. The *Star* puts Diana on the cover because the working girls and hausfraus who buy it want to see it. NBC News wants a piece of that Oprah demographic, so Tom Brokaw pretends that it's news, too. Hey -- you gotta put *something* between the commercials, right?

There was a time when newsrooms were run by people who made judgments about what ought to be news, not what people would pay to read. That era ended long ago, and its death was reaffirmed when "legitimate" news organizations began using the tabloids to break stories so that they could put Dick Morris and Gennifer Flowers on their front pages, too.

Now that the paparazzi are under fire, news editors are pretending they never heard of them: "Why, we would never run those awful photos in our paper...until someone else does, anyway."

It's all part of the game. I'll take complete irrelevance and crocodile tears for whatever they're worth. Today they look like a sure winner.

God's Punchline

September, 1997

Two wire reports appeared on the same day:

"Accepting the Nobel in the name of the 'unwanted, unloved and uncared for,' Mother Teresa wore the same $1 white sari that she had adopted to identify herself with the poor when she founded her order, Missionaries of Charity. Wherever people needed comfort, she was there: among the hungry in Ethiopia, the radiation victims at Chernobyl, the rubble of Armenia's earthquake, in the squalid townships of South Africa. One day in 1948, she found a woman 'half eaten up by maggots and rats' lying in the street in front of a Calcutta hospital, and sat with the woman until she died."

"Seventy percent of viewers polled by the tabloid TV show American Journal said Princess Diana should be awarded the Nobel Peace Prize for her humanitarian work."

There is a God, and he is laughing.

He has played cosmic paparazzo, using a flashbulb irony to catch the entire human race at its most petty, pompous and self-deluded. And most of you didn't even smile.

My theory is that Mother Teresa, who had been in ill health for years, was originally slated to become lead soprano in the Choir Invisible months ago. But God, who loves nothing more than a good joke, booked her on the celestial equivalent of USAir to ensure a late departure. Thanks to His immaculate sense of comic timing, Mother Teresa roared to Heaven right over Di-Fest, like a low-flying 747 drowning out the wailing below.

Only Americans have become deaf to irony. Everyone who got up at four in the morning to watch the funeral, who wore out TV remotes clicking from one prime-time special to the next, who thought Princess

Diana's demise received an appropriate level of press coverage -- these people don't realize they've just been had.

It's a gag, a joke, folks -- and you're it. As the kids say: You are SO busted!

Oh, you thought you were safe, indulging in the shameless excess of the Royal Death, playing along with this real-life edition of "Oprah Meets Dallas." After all, wasn't everyone else playing along, too?

You felt free to say aloud that Lady Di deserves sainthood -- after all, hadn't she once shaken hands with an AIDS patient? And one wearing polyester at the time, too (ooooh!)

And Diana sacrificed so much happiness to raise those two fine sons (though not quite enough to stay in an unhappy marriage), despite the daily hardships she faced: living in a castle, being a multi-millionaire, having a staff of full-time nannies, finding time to pick up the latest from Armani...

"How does a single mother do it?" you wondered aloud.

So you wept along, obsessed along, played along, rationalizing it all by saying that Princess Di deserved the wave of overwrought media mourning. She was unique. There was no one else like her.

Then ... WHAM! The Cosmic Cream Pie. The so-called tragedy of Di's life put in instant perspective when compared to the life of Mother Teresa. The celebrity-struck goons who whooped up Di's occasional visit to an elementary school sounded painfully boorish as the media quietly reported the life work of a woman who founded leper colonies.

If all the self-indulgent, Elton-esque tears shed for Diana Spencer -- whose celebrated accomplishments amounted to giving other people's money to charity and breaking up a couple of marriages -- could have been shed for Mother Teresa, the Saint of the Gutter herself would have been embarrassed.

Watching them shed for the Saint of Saks Fifth Avenue was almost unbearable.

I will confess enough personal naiveté about the human condition to expect that Mother Teresa's death might slow down the national Digasm, or at least reduce it to low moanings.

Silly me. In most media outlets, Mother Teresa was the second lead, bumped by more pressing news involving which color socks Prince William would wear while following the royal hearse.

Jehovah's joke went right over our heads. We are all lost in the Era of Oprah: We demand crying queens, people's princesses and mob-fearing monarchs who genuflect before the readers of the *National Inquirer*.

The true nobility of a life like Mother Teresa's means nothing to us. When was she ever on the cover of *Vogue*? How many naughty phone calls did she make from Buckingham Palace? When did she ever auction off an old dress for charity, and what would she get for it, anyway -- a buck?

Diana Spencer had a higher calling. Many believe she was the only hope of saving the British monarchy, quite a feat given that Britain has been ruled by a parliament for quite a while now. Others believe she was the most beautiful woman in the world -- a claim that might seem true in England -- but a casual glance through *Cosmo* puts that notion to rest.

But Diana's true higher calling was to be the first martyr of the Oprah Era, the first celebrity to die whose entire celebrity was self-contained. Diana was famous simply for being famous.

And Mother Teresa? It was once believed that a lifetime of sacrifice for others would be rewarded with honor at your death and beyond. I cannot speak for the hereafter, but our children -- watching the difference in reaction to the death of a plastic, pop icon and a true humanitarian -- can see clearly what we treasure more.

Impeach Reno

September, 1997

On April 19, 1993, government agents raided a Branch Davidian compound near Waco, Texas, killing about 80 men, women and children and leaving just one survivor: Janet Reno.

How this spectacled incompetent kept her job after perhaps the single worst law enforcement debacle in American history is a mystery. You usually have to be a member of the teacher's union to be this incompetent and not get fired for it.

As Attorney General, Janet Reno is part of a long line of "bad babes" serving in the Clinton administration. Hazel O'Leary, the soon-to-be indicted head of the Department of Energy, was flying herself around the world on a luxury tour jet. She has since been caught with her hand in the cookie jar.

And when Surgeon General Dr. Joyceln Elders wasn't promoting masturbation in our middle schools, she was doing her part to keep Bill Clinton in the same back pages of the history books as the Harding or Polk administrations.

Add to this Janet Reno. Attorney General Reno is supposed to be the watchdog in the government, making sure everyone plays by the rules. While her physical appearance may enhance the "watchdog" image, in fact the Clintons have walked over her like a cheap rug. And she lies there and takes it. Consider the record:

The Clintons take office and immediately order all of the U.S. Attorneys to be sacked -- including the one investigating Whitewater -- and Janet Reno obediently passes out the pink slips. No questions, no complaints.

The Clintons get their hands on the FBI files of 900 political opponents, and Janet Reno can't find anything worth prosecuting. A group of Americans are unprotected while their government passes around their FBI files like a bottle of Boone's Farm at a high school party, and Janet Reno doesn't lift a finger.

Documents subpoenaed by law enforcement for two years mysteriously reappear in the White House, practically on Hillary Clinton's nightstand, and Janet Reno mutters something about "things like that always turn up in the last place you look..."

And now we have Buddhist monks with prosecutorial immunity. Try running that one through your First Amendment Rights-O-Meter.

During the 1996 campaign, Al Gore visited a Buddhist temple in California filled with devotees who had taken a vow of poverty. Miraculously (hey, they're monks), the impoverished acolytes were able to scrape together few hundred grand for Vice President Gore.

When it was discovered that this group of impoverished monks were laundering money for the Democratic National Committee, Al Gore did what politicians do: He lied. He claimed he didn't know the event was a fund-raiser, even though his staff covered his desk with more disclaimers than a pack of cigarettes.

The problem isn't Al Gore's lying: That's his job. The problem is when the chief law-enforcement officer lets him get away with it. Janet Reno's refusal to name a special prosecutor to investigate the White House fundraising scandal is a new low, even by Washington standards. We know there was money laundering, we know Mr. Gore has lied about his conduct, we know that he solicited money on government property -- just by watching CNN.

Janet Reno is such a poor prosecutor that her crack investigative team had to find out that Al Gore was raising money for himself inside the Oval Office by reading it in the morning paper.

She's a watchdog who won't bark, a bloodhound who won't tree. Janet Reno is a disgrace, and she should go.

Now, many of you are already yawning: "Who cares if the law was broken? So Clinton-Gore are dishonest -- oh, that's a news flash." You are right, of course. The American people, taken as a whole, couldn't care less about the rule of law. They want justice and revenge served up on Court TV. If it doesn't involve homicide or hanky-panky, the people just won't care.

That's why it is particularly important to have a law enforcement officer who does care, especially when no one else does. Being obnoxious in defense of the law is no vice.

When the Hillary Hounds start baying that these campaign laws are minor (these are the same whiners who want to execute people guilty of unauthorized smoking), someone needs to look them in the eye and say, "The law is the law -- change it, don't break it."

Think, for example, of the 55 m.p.h. speed limit. Fifty-five on the interstate was about as easy to enforce as the "six inch" rule at a Catholic school dance. Should our sheriffs have had the policy of letting their buddies off the hook because nobody liked the law?

No, we want the law enforced. We also want our political leaders to change the laws that don't work. If campaign finance laws need to be reformed (I certainly think so), then get Congress to change the law. Only Janet Reno could argue with a straight face that the Clinton administration supports tough, new campaign laws when they were unwilling to obey the old, lax ones.

Janet Reno's scorched-earth policy of incompetence and cronyism continues long after Waco. It is long past time for the Congress to impeach her and bring it to an end.

These Kids Today

August, 1997

"My mom's just going to have to take me shopping." -- A New Mexico high schooler, sporting spiked hair and a dog collar, sent home for violating a new statewide school dress code.

Once upon a time, the last refuge of the scoundrel was patriotism. Today it is day care.

Whenever some elected official or self-proclaimed public advocate is about to seize a chunk of my personal liberty or spare change (usually both), they inevitably justify this abuse as a social necessity "for the children." Like battered wives of a bygone era, we are urged to suffer silently for the sake of the kids.

Well, with two screaming brats of my own, I prefer to do my suffering at home, thanks just the same. So when the Smoke Nazis or the Internet Nannies lobby me to join their children's crusades, I politely tell them: "I gave at the ovum."

Pro-child public policy is almost inevitably a disaster. It was the motivating force behind the single most stupid piece of legislation ever passed by the U.S. Congress (and that's no small feat): Prohibition.

Believe it or not, youngsters, in 1920 a majority of Americans voted to make it illegal to manufacture or sell alcohol in these United States. How did that happen?

Historians have many theories (mine being that most people were too drunk at the time to know what they were voting for), but without a doubt one primary motivation was to protect children from the evils of demon rum.

The American electorate decided it wasn't fair that some kids had dads who couldn't hold their liquor, who drank up the milk money and neglected their fatherly duties. To protect these unfortunate offspring, the people of America -- never too thrilled with the idea of individual liberty to begin with -- took away the freedom to drink from every responsible adult in our land.

Our nation promptly got hammered by the giddy effects of the law of unintended consequences.

While alcohol consumption did decline, perhaps by as much as a third, much of the nation was overwhelmed by bootlegging, lawlessness and gangland violence. A new criminal class was created that was far more dangerous than a drunken dad stumbling home from the local pub.

Prohibition failed as a policy, but it succeeded in raising a national question that remains unanswered: How bad do you let things get in your neighbor's house before you kick down the door?

After all, Prohibition may have been a bad solution, but drunkenness was a very real problem. In communities across America, children with loving fathers who helped them with their schoolwork lived next door to dead-drunk dads who came home every night and kicked anything under three feet tall.

This inequity in the quality of parents continues today. Take our young friend in New Mexico who was sent home from school because Mom didn't put her in a regulation dog collar. This spike-haired student probably sits across the aisle from some Mormon classmate dressed in Osmond-Wear, whose mom makes her drink eight glasses of milk a day and sends her to bed before the Family Viewing Hour is over. Is this fair? One kid's being groomed for great success and the other checked for fleas -- is that right?

Yes, actually, it is.

It is only fair that kids with concerned, involved parents have better lives than kids who don't. If you spend the night before the algebra test reviewing logarithms with your little Einstein and I spend it teaching

Junior the drum solo from "In A Goddidavida," there should be a difference in the outcome. That's only fair.

This is the equity of inequity, the justice of injustice. Sure, we all wish every child could have Donna Reed and Mr. Rogers for parents, but all too often they get, well...us.

Dress codes, curfews, taxpayer-funded day care -- these are inherently unfair attempts to level the playing field between good parents and bad. Look around at the adults you know and the parents they have, and you'll agree that most of us get the parents we deserve.

Most, but not all. I may tend towards libertarianism, but I have no problem with the government taking kids out of homes where they are starved, abused, or exposed to Howard Stern. We have to draw the line somewhere.

For example, there was the horrible death of Christina Corrigan, the 700-lb. 13-year-old so obese she couldn't get up and go to the bathroom. Young Christina spent her days lying on a sheet in front of the television and eating herself to death because "Christina demanded food and I usually gave in." That's what her mother told the police after her daughter died of heart failure in the living room.

"It took six people to roll Christina's body onto a sheet of canvas and drag it to the coroner's wagon," the AP reported. And you have to wonder if any of the six ever turned to the mother and said, "Two words, lady -- Jenny Craig!"

This child didn't eat herself to death -- she was fed to death. If you're too fat to make it to the bathroom, chances are you won't be jogging down to the corner grocery, either. A person so big they can't get up and feed themselves is, by definition, on a diet -- the Somalia diet. And unless you can lure a passing cat onto the hibachi, you're going to lose weight.

I believe Christina's mother is the model for the new child-first movement. As a mom, she was willing to suffer continuously --

working full-time and taking care of an unnecessarily immobile daughter. But she wasn't strong enough to put her daughter through the relatively mild pangs of a Big Mac attack.

Most American children could use a bit more suffering, a bit more social policy neglect.

And more parents could use a good, stiff drink.

The Life of Riley

September, 1997

President Clinton has been criticized, and rightly so, for the cut-rate quality of his Cabinet members. Reno, Shalala, Reich, they all have an "off-the-rack" quality about them, even in their appearance. The whole bunch looks like they fell out of the irregular bin at T. J. Maxx.

However, one cabinet member who certainly fits this description has somehow escaped harsh scrutiny: South Carolina's former governor and the current U.S. Secretary of Education, Dick Riley.

Given the Palmetto State's horrible school system, choosing a former South Carolina governor to head the Education Department is like naming Dennis Rodman president of the Southern Baptist Convention. This is doubly true for Dick Riley, whose term began with South Carolina dead last in education, and ended with a huge education tax increase... and South Carolina dead last in education.

Whatever it was President Clinton saw in our governor, it managed to escape the poor suckers stuck in South Carolina's crummy school system.

A point of personal privilege: Bill Clinton has a thing for failed S.C. politicos. For example, before Clinton chose him to head the Democratic National Committee and Chinese Money Laundromat, Don Fowler was state chairman of the South Carolina Democratic Party. When Fowler took over the state party, Democrats controlled eight of the nine constitutional offices and had a 4-2 majority in our congressional delegation. When Fowler left to join Clinton's team, the Republicans held eight of the nine Constitutional offices and had a 4-2 majority in Congress.

Speaking for Republicans everywhere: Don Fowler is my kind of Democrat!

Anyway, the appointment of Dick Riley to the Department of Education has been frequently overlooked, perhaps because the Department of Education is so overlookable. Less than 10 percent of public education spending is federal, and most of that is either for kids of military families or special education.

Nevertheless, Secretary Riley loves nothing more than to pontificate on the state of education in America, and he was recently back in the Palmetto State to discuss pedagogy in all its aspects.

His first, and most surprising, pronunciamento was that "South Carolina is ready for a new renaissance" in education.

Not to split hairs with America's top educator, but before one can have a renaissance, don't you have to have a "naissance?" If South Carolina ever enjoyed a golden age of intellectual achievement in our public schools, I must have slept in that day. Given my home state's academic tradition of viewing books as a good way to get the fire nice and hot before you add the cross, what era of enlightenment is Secretary Riley urging us to return to? The invention of the cotton gin? The invention of the wheel?

Riley made this comment at a meeting of the National Association of State Boards of Education on Kiawah Island, where attending bureaucrats strolled our lovely Lowcountry beaches thanks to the generosity of taxpayers back home. The bureaucrats running America's failing education system may have had cushy surroundings, but Riley's speech contained tough words and harsh criticism.

Not of them, of course. No, the harsh words were for me.

Not by name, but I am a proponent of school choice, and as such I apparently have upset the Secretary:

"I am most distressed by some of the overheated rhetoric some are using to mischaracterize public education today, usually when they are promoting the silver bullet solution of vouchers," Riley said.

"When they talk and talk and talk about vouchers, they're not interested in constructive criticism of our schools, how we can make them better and improve them. They continually demean public education. They belittle our children, our parents and our teachers. I tell you, I am tired of it," he said.

Secretary Riley's comments have caused me to amend one of the world's most famous maxims: "Those who can, do. Those who can't, teach. Those who can't tell the difference get to run the schools."

As a graduate of South Carolina's public schools, and as an observer of its current graduates, I can't imagine how it is possible to "mischaracterize public education" in any way that would be worse than the truth. The only way to "overheat" the rhetoric regarding Riley's government-run school system would be to accuse teachers of secretly administering lobotomies to unsuspecting students.

Given the pathetic state of South Carolina schools, why is Secretary Riley angry that parents are looking for alternatives? Riley says that people like me, who believe parents should be able to pick the best school for their individual children, that we "belittle our children, our parents." This is clearly backwards. The only reason to deny children and parents the right to choose is because you think they are too stupid to pick the right schools.

Secretary Riley's logic is sloppy, his arguments flawed, his conclusions disingenuous. If that doesn't make him an ideal member of the Clinton Cabinet, I can't imagine what would.

White House Follies

November, 1997

If nothing else, the Clintons certainly keep American politics entertaining. First fund-raising coffees, then sleep-overs and now, home movies! It's like having Uncle Darryl and Aunt Vergie running our federal government, except that President Clinton rarely wanders into the front yard in his boxers to pick up the morning paper.

Life in the White House has been so ridiculous for so long that events which once would have stopped the presses are now buried in the back pages of the paper. Months ago, when Hillary Clinton's long-lost billing records appeared on her nightstand two years after they had been subpoenaed, eyebrows were raised.

Today, videotapes long sought by the courts miraculously spring from the world's most well-monitored monitoring system, and no one bats an eye. "Uh, we just kinda found 'em under the sofa," is the White House explanation for how videos of presidential fundraisers remained conveniently undiscovered until well after the 1996 election.

To which I reply: Are you kidding? Ever since the Oval Office recording system brought Nixon down, you can't get an unauthorized piece of *Scotch* tape into the White House. But you couldn't find a stack of presidential videos?

This lame excuse turned laughable when paid White House stooge Lanny Davis insisted that the military-run White House Communications Agency that made the tapes couldn't find them in computer archive searches because nobody thought to look under the heading "coffees."

"Damn! Why didn't I think of that," Janet Reno must be saying to herself...

Janet Reno is far more clever at finding ways to avoid prosecuting the president's friends than she is at finding evidence with which to indict them. President Clinton is also better at demanding stronger campaign finance laws than he is at obeying the ones we have today.

And, despite what you see on the nightly news, there is an enforceable campaign finance law in place. But don't take my word for it. Just ask Robert B. Maloney.

Bob Maloney is a former Smith Barney broker who laundered money into his brother's 1994 congressional campaign. He did this by asking friends to write checks to his brother, then he personally reimbursed them for the money donated. Nineteen people wrote checks for some $39,000, all of which Mr. Maloney made good out of his own pocket.

What happened to Bob Maloney? He was indicted this week and faces a maximum of one year in prison and a $100,000 fine on each of the 17 misdemeanor counts filed against him.

But somehow, the same law that reaches Bob Maloney doesn't quite extend to the leaders of the free world. Al Gore's famous fundraiser at a Buddhist monastery in California (motto: "How To Turn Your Vow Of Poverty Into Cold, Hard Cash!") was an identical money-laundering scheme.

The record is clear and undisputed: Penniless monks handed over thousands of other's people dollars, and they got checks back from big-dollar donors who were breaking the law. But while Bob Maloney sits in stir, Al Gore is still fundraising.

Interestingly, Mr. Gore's case is actually a stronger one for prosecutors because there is a specific law prohibiting political fundraising at religious institutions. But these laws didn't stop the Clinton-Gore money machine.

And how bizarre is it to watch lefty Hillary-types attacking the Promise Keepers for the mere possibility of mixing religion and politics, while they continue to defend Al Gore and his confirmed political activity at a temple of worship?

This is what I mean by the complete lack of integrity. Their hypocrisy and self-serving self-righteousness seems to pervade the entire government. The fact that Bill Clinton and Al Gore are, as people, wholly corrupt isn't as disturbing to me as the corrupting influence they are having on the people around them.

Even the normal bureaucratic functions of government, which inadvertently promote individual liberty through incompetence and inefficiency, have broken down altogether. It doesn't necessarily bother me that the FBI is so inefficient it can't find home movies of White House fundraisers. What bothers me is that this same FBI was conveniently just competent enough to hand over their background files on Clinton's enemies.

This double standard of justice is the new twist to old-fashioned political corruption added by the Clinton administration. It's one thing if Janet Reno takes a laissez-faire attitude toward all fundraising violations. It's something else altogether when the Bob Maloneys of the world go to jail and the Al Gores go to the Democratic National Convention.

Chapter 4

"I Did Not Have Sex With That Woman"

End of The Presidency

January, 1998

Writing about a fast-breaking news story like the Clinton White House Intern Scandal for a weekly publication is inherently dangerous. In the days between my writing and your reading, virtually anything could happen in this rollercoaster ride of a presidency, and it probably will. However, I can make one statement today with absolute confidence: By the time you read this, the Clinton presidency will be over.

I can make this assertion because, in fact, the Clinton presidency is already over. Yes, he may still be sitting in the office, trying to inconspicuously sneak peeks into the blouses of mail room staffers, but Bill Clinton's tenure as president is finished.

A man who has been caught having sex in the White House with a 21-year-old employee and lying about it under oath simply cannot be president. The media won't let him, and neither will the people of America.

"Aha," Clinton apologists violently assert, "but he hasn't been caught. Nothing has been proven!" And it may never be "proven," the key word in Mrs. Clinton's *Today* show hatchet job on Kenneth Starr, because the president's defenders are not using the usual standard of

71

reasonable doubt. They are instead using the newly developed O.J. Simpson standard of "possible doubt."

Is it possible that aliens beamed down to Earth, put on O.J.'s socks and then murdered his wife? Theoretically, yes. But every reasonable person knows that O.J. Simpson is a murderer and that President Clinton had sex with a 21-year-old intern. There is no room for reasonable doubt.

The clincher for me, by the way, was the revelation that the president had called Ms. Lewinsky at home. Do you have any idea how hard it is for the president of the United States to make a phone call? As a general rule, presidents are only allowed to call people who can blow things up, or (in a new twist added by this president) write very large checks to the Democratic National Committee. So until someone steps forward with proof that Monica Lewinsky had a sack of cash from Charlie Trie or a thermo-nuclear device hidden in her sock drawer, we can all rest assured that she and the president had a sexual relationship.

Why else would a married, middle-aged man call a 21-year-old girl? Phone chess?

The Clintonistas will no doubt continue to slander Kenneth Starr, Linda Tripp, etc., etc, but to no avail. By his own actions, the President has ended his service because there are at least three things a person must be able to do to be president, and Bill Clinton can no longer do them.

The first is communicate with the nation. A president must have the ability to hold a press conference with other heads of state that doesn't invoke puns on the phrase "head of state." He must also be able to make a simple public statement, such as "I never had sexual relations with that woman," without having every member of the press corps whip out a thesaurus and begin speculating what he really meant.

This president is in the bizarre situation of having to explain his explanations because of his well-established ability to slip through invisible loopholes. Remember: He still believes that he did not lie when he denied having an affair with Gennifer Flowers even though he had sex with her. And I hesitate to even repeat the theories on the President's contorted view of sexuality which allows him to deny Ms. Lewinsky's charges. As of today, Mr. Clinton's defense can best be summarized by that classic argument of trailer-park lawyering, "Eatin' Ain't Cheatin'."

Another essential presidential task is the ability to declare war. Constitutionally, no one else in America can do so, and politically, President Clinton cannot do so. Why? Because our nation will not follow a man into war whose public policy would then be described as "killing our sons and screwing our daughters."

Finally, the Clinton presidency is over because, as much as I love a good laugh, no person can withstand the avalanche of ridicule this pathetic putz has pulled down upon his own head. Americans have a tacit understanding with their elected officials: "Go ahead, take the perks, hire a personal stenographer to sit in your lap, send a little government gravy to your golf buddies from the old law firm, that's fine. Just don't embarrass me. Don't make me feel humiliated that I voted for you."

President Clinton has broken the deal. Every public statement he makes from now on will be somebody's punchline. Soon, the joke will get old, and President Clinton will lose every politician's most important asset: the ability to entertain.

And we, the people will give President Clinton the hook. He may still have the desk, but he won't have the job.

The fact is, with all the Clintonistas screaming that "this isn't Watergate," President Clinton passed the Watergate standard long ago. Obstruction of justice? Why do you think President Clinton's friends paid Webb Hubbell more money to stay in jail and keep his mouth shut then he could earn as a private attorney?

Perjury and obstruction of justice? This is a White House where subpoenaed documents mysteriously appear on the First Lady's nightstand, where long-sought videotapes of presidential fundraisers with Chinese arms dealers are suddenly "discovered" after the 1996 election.

Abuse of power? In both Travelgate and Filegate, the FBI was used to punish political enemies of the president: The White House travel office director was wrongly indicted (and later acquitted) by the Clinton Justice Department, and I trust we all remember Craig Livingstone, the "useful galoot" who no one will admit to having hired, but who somehow was able to compile the supposedly confidential FBI files of hundreds of Republicans.

The president's problem today is not that he has violated the Nixon standard -- that's old news. No, the president's in trouble because he finally broke the Oprah barrier, because he is engaged in a scandal that stupid people can understand.

It's a safe bet in politics that when you become a potential guest for Jerry Springer ("My Lesbian Wife Ordered Our New Dog to Eat Subpoenaed Documents!"), your presidency is over.

Once again, I am writing in the very midst of the thrashing storm. By the time you've read this, it may have already blown over. If, for example, the president has the courage to do the right thing, he will formally resign from office, and he will do so in the next few days.

Then again, if Bill Clinton were a man of personal integrity and courage, my column this week would be about the Super Bowl.

President O.J.

February, 1998

"There's never been anything like it." --President Bill Clinton on the *trial of O.J. Simpson, 1994.*

Until now.

William Jefferson Clinton has become the Oranthal James Simpson of American politics: Everyone knows he did it; we're just watching to see if he can get away with it.

Will he? If he does, he will have successfully walked a path hewn through the American justice system by pioneers like Johnnie Cochran and Robert Shapiro just three years ago. In fact, a review of the two cases, taken directly from news reports, shows that President Clinton and O.J. Simpson are sharing virtually the same defense strategies. Legally speaking, it looks like a case of "Separated at Birth."

THE O.J./CLINTON DEFENSE STRATEGIES

"DENY, DENY, DENY."

"I did not have sex with that woman, Ms. Lewinsky."--*President Clinton.*

"Absolutely, 100 percent not guilty"--*O.J. Simpson.*

"IT'S A CONSPIRACY."

After Judge Ito blocks all but two of L.A. Detective Mark Fuhrman's racial slurs from testimony, defense lawyer Johnnie Cochran accuses Ito of being part of a police conspiracy to frame Simpson.

First Lady Hillary Clinton claims Monica Lewinsky is part of a "vast, right-wing conspiracy" to frame her husband.

Cochran calls the prosecution's introduction of O.J.'s wife-beating into testimony a "clear and orchestrated attempt to influence public opinion."

Referring to the activities of Ken Starr's office, White House spokesman Joe Lockhart says, "It seems to be an orchestrated campaign of misinformation."

Cochran threatens to call an ex-FBI agent who testified in the World Trade Center bombing case that he had been forced to doctor evidence. The agent had no connection whatsoever with the Simpson case.

White House aids tell *Newsweek* -- without offering evidence -- that the "talking point" document that corroborates Lewinsky's taped account is fabricated.

"HEY, NOBODY'S PERFECT!"

"He, like all of us, has made mistakes. Of course, we know that only one perfect person has ever walked the earth."--*Johnnie Cochran.*

One aide speaking on condition of anonymity, said Clinton particularly was buoyed by Scripture referrals offered by ministers supporting the President. The references included: Romans 3:23, "For all have sinned and come short of the glory of God," and John, Chapter 8, in which Jesus said, "Let he who is without sin cast the first stone."

"I'M THE VICTIM OF A POWERFUL PROSECUTOR."

Cochran complains that the prosecutors have more resources than the defense, though prosecution lawyers earned $45 per hour while the Dream Team members were making $650-$700 per hour.

Clinton defenders claim Ken Starr's office has spent $30 million (or $40 or $50 million, depending on which day you ask) as part of a partisan campaign to get the president after years of failing to prove the original Whitewater allegations.

Defense expert Frederic Rieders, who told jurors a patently lame story about blood possibly being planted on O.J.'s socks, responds to cross-examination by attacking the prosecution: "I've been pestered by the prosecution from hell to breakfast."

White House aides accuse Starr's investigators of using inappropriate and possibly illegal tactics to pressure potential witnesses.

"YOU CAN'T TRUST MY ACCUSERS."

Cochran points out several times that Detective Tom Lange lives in Simi Valley -- the white suburb where LAPD officers had recently been found "not guilty" in connection with the Rodney King beating -- implying that this raises issues about his character.

Clinton defenders frequently note that Linda Tripp was part of the Bush administration and is a friend of a right-wing book agent who worked for Richard Nixon.

Defense attorneys maintain they will not play the race card, then denounce Detective Fuhrman as a white supremacist who planted evidence to frame Simpson.

Despite assurances from White House spokeswoman Ann Lewis that the administration would not attack Ms. Lewinsky's character, a White House aide calls reporters to offer information about Monica's sexual past, her weight problems and what the aide said was her nickname - "The Stalker." She was known as a flirt who wore her skirts too short and was "a little bit weird."

"YOU'LL NEVER PROVE IT."

Before being arrested, O.J. spent several days at the home of his friend Robert Kardashian, discussing his troubles. When O.J. escaped the police and fled for Mexico in his infamous white Bronco, Kardashian then paid the fees required to become reinstated as an attorney in California, thus allowing him to invoke privilege and avoid testifying against his friend regarding their pre-arrest conversations.

President Clinton is considering invoking executive privilege to keep attorneys in the White House from testifying against him.

When police tried to get documents regarding O.J.'s wife-beating from the defendant's office, they were blocked by the defense. When the officers returned later, O.J.'s assistant had shredded them.

The White House has refused to release copies of entry logs and phone records which could confirm that Ms. Lewinsky met with the President privately after December 25th, which would mean he had committed perjury. (No report on whether or not they've been shredded yet.)

Forensic expert Henry Lee, who went on to dispute much of the prosecution's blood evidence, was at Kardashian's house with O.J. and A.C. Cowlings the night before O.J.'s attempted escape.

President Clinton met alone with Monica Lewinsky on December 28, just before she turned in her sworn deposition attempting to deny her affair with the President.

"I REALLY WANT TO TELL MY STORY..."

"The majority view on the defense team is that Simpson should testify. O.J. wants to testify, too." --*Johnny Cochran.*

President Clinton acknowledged there were legitimate questions about his relationship with Monica Lewinsky and that "the American people have a right to get answers. I want to do that. I'd like for you have more rather than less, sooner rather than later."

"...BUT I WON'T."

O.J. Simpson never took the stand in his own defense.

"I'm honoring the rules of the investigation" by refusing to provide details of his relationship with Ms. Lewinsky, Clinton said. A spokesperson later acknowledged that there were no "rules" prohibiting the President from explaining his relationship with Monica, other than the rules of "common sense."

Neither O.J. Simpson's attorneys or the President's representatives mentioned the Fifth Amendment right against self-incrimination.

Thinking With Your Clinton

February, 1998

The voice that joyously leapt at me from the phone was very familiar. But the words took me by surprise. "Michael, this Clinton sex thing -- isn't it great!?"

It was a friend of mine, a college buddy now finishing his med-school residency. Years after college we still talked frequently, but I couldn't recall him ever uttering a single sentence about politics, even though I work as a political consultant. Bright, entertaining, informed, sure -- but as far as I could tell, he didn't know the difference between Richard Nixon and Richard Dawson.

President Clinton had changed all that. "Are you following this Monica story?" he went on excitedly. "It is absolutely amazing!"

But when I asked him when he had joined me in the ranks of Clinton-bashers, he stopped me cold. "Clinton-*basher*? No, no, Michael. I'm not bashing the President. He's going to get away with it, and I think it's wonderful!"

I didn't want to sound like Bill Bennett thumping on a copy of the *Book of Virtues*, but I found it difficult to share his enthusiasm. I told him the silver lining around the public's current celebration of presidential perjury had not yet caught my eye.

"Are you kidding me, Michael? This Clinton guy is a godsend! Here we are, you and I, a couple of guys in our mid-to-late thirties, with middle age staring us coldly in the face. And the President of the United States has just made it okay for older guys to screw around with younger women! We are on the verge of a new sexual revolution and with you and me as the target demographic! And I say it's about damn time."

"Think about it this way," he went on. "Guys our age missed the 1960s free love movement. We missed the permissive 1970s, too. When we finally hit the sexual dance floor, so did the AIDS virus. We're the generation who had to deal with HIV before we even got around to heavy petting. I thought we were doomed. And now -- we're the Clinton Generation! Is America a great country or what?"

I started to explain that the story was far from over, that there were more political peaks and valleys ahead, but he stopped me.

"Michael, when the boat's a rockin', don't start knockin'! Why fight it? Women's attitudes have completely changed, almost overnight. There are a bunch of feminists where I work who just last week were ready to turn a lingering glance into a lawsuit. I went to work yesterday, and they've decided it's okay to be a dirty old man! Medical interns who used to be a harassment filing waiting to happen now eye me with a look of expectation.

"We're on a teeter-totter, with President Clinton on one side and every moral conclusion of the history of western civilization on the other, and Bill's winning! You the man, Bill! You the man!"

I tried again to argue that the president might, in fact, pay a political price when the facts reveal -- as they almost certainly will -- that he did have sex with his 21-year-old intern and lied about it, but my friend laughed in my face.

"You think the nation's moral character is going to bring Bill Clinton down? Michael, you've got it backwards! Instead of demanding he rise to our level, virtually every college-educated woman I know is ready to drop down to his! And, buddy, I mean 'drop down' in a very literal sense..."

My doctor-in-training was on a roll. "And I ask you, Michael, who are we to judge? Hey, he's the president; I'm a resident. Besides, instead of condemning his failings, you and I should cheer him on. We're going to be the big winners. A few more years of President Clinton, and Woody Allen can get elected pope!

"In fact," he continued, "that's why I called. On behalf of every middle-aged married man -- and those of us headed for middle age and probably marriage in the all-too-near future -- I want to start a 'Draft Clinton!' movement and elect the president to another term. Can you help me?"

I pointed out that, if he was serious, he first needed to change the name of his movement. After all, the last time someone tried to draft Bill Clinton, he fled to Europe. I also noted that the United States Constitution prohibits presidents from serving more then two terms.

"Yeah, yeah, yeah," he answered. "And 50-year-old married men aren't supposed to fondle the office help, either. Michael, you're still thinking under the old paradigm. Don't you understand? Aren't you paying attention? The president of the United States met privately with a witness who had been subpoenaed to testify against him, afterwards she changes her story and lies under oath, then his pals get her a high-paying job for which she is clearly not qualified...and nobody cares! It's a whole new world!"

He had a point. I suppose President Clinton could claim that he had never actually served his first term. You know, he could say someone else had been president from 1993-1997 and all the videotape and news stories about him in Oval Office were Republican fabrications...

"Now you're thinking with your Clinton!" he shouted. "That's it. He can look right in the camera and tell the American people: 'I never served as president before 1996 -- these allegations are false.' Hell, no one even has to believe him! We all want Bill to be president -- the American people couldn't care less about the facts. And Hillary can say anyone who disagrees is part of a vast, right-wing conspiracy."

There might even be a legal loophole, I went on. The president can claim he was never officially sworn in the first time. He can say that when they administered the oath of office in 1993, he thought it was a federal deposition and so he lied.

"Now you've got it. Look, I gotta go. A couple of young coeds have asked me to give them some career advice and, being the sensitive, gregarious guy I am, I'm heading over to counsel them in a friend's Jacuzzi. But if anyone can figure out how we can get President Clinton elected for a third term, you can.

"Just remember: If you give the American people a choice between the integrity of the U.S. Constitution or a sycophantic politician who appeals to our lowest, neediest elements of human nature and will tell us whatever we want to hear -- we'll be in like Flynn! Life is good, my friend!"

And then he hung up, another idealistic American inspired to action by President Clinton.

Dead Kennedys

January, 1998

"I am famous. I achieved in one day what it took Robert Kennedy his whole life to accomplish."-- Sirhan Sirhan, after assassinating RFK in 1968.

It is ironic that both Michael Kennedy and Sirhan Sirhan are famous for precisely the same two reasons: a lifetime of accomplishments by Robert Kennedy, and a single, shameful act of their own.

Sirhan Sirhan has no identity outside his relationship to RFK. In 1968, in the kitchen of a Los Angeles hotel, Sirhan took his place in the hall of eternal infamy. Up to that moment, he was as unknown to the average American as your run-of-the-mill busboy, sewer worker or vice president of the United States.

The same could be said of the recently self-bludgeoned Michael Kennedy, one of the hundreds of nameless, faceless Kennedys who thrive in the cold, amoral environs of New England. One year ago, Michael Kennedy's death on an Aspen ski slope would have been minor news -- a one-paragraph "brief" tucked away in the holiday newspapers next to other unread stories like "Locations for Recycling Your Christmas Tree" and "Celebrating Ramadan in the American South."

Just one year later, NBC News literally interrupts this program to tell us that Michael had George-Of-The-Jungled himself to that Great Kennedy Compound in the Sky. The networks dusted off their "Di-Cams" to broadcast his funeral live, with hush-breathed commentary about Carolyn Kennedy's clothes. Weekend talk shows gave non-stop analysis, going so far as to find women in Massachusetts who had not been propositioned by a Kennedy, drunk or sober. Even in our local papers, Michael Kennedy's funeral made the same number of front-page appearances as Mother Teresa's.

Clinton and Me

Why the change? How did Michael Kennedy go from minor media memo to front-page mega-event?

Michael Kennedy was a child molester.

That's it. That is the only difference between the Michael Kennedy of New Year's Eve, 1996 and the man whose funeral aired live this week.

One year ago, he was a Kennedy, one of the 10 surviving children of RFK. One year ago, he was head of a non-profit corporation providing heating fuel to poor people.

And one year ago, Michael Kennedy was the "extraordinarily effective" campaign manager now eulogized by Democratic hack Mary Anne Marsh, who gushed: "He won every race he ever managed, which is more than most people can say in this business." Not to speak ill of the dead, but getting Kennedys elected in Massachusetts is about as impressive as getting rednecks elected in South Carolina.

And Michael Kennedy's campaign record was not without blemish. In August, his brother Joe Kennedy withdrew from the Massachusetts governor's race, in part because campaign manager Michael was caught helping the babysitter with some of the more hands-on portions of her biology homework.

In the world of Democrat political consultants, nailing your 14-year-old neighbor may or may not be as tacky as hiring a toe-sucking prostitute, but even Dick Morris' clients weren't driven out of public service.

Regardless, none of these accomplishments, real or imagined were significant enough to generate the mini-tidal wave of media reaction. Michael Kennedy was on your TV screen for an entire week because -- and only because -- he seduced a child, because there were political consequences to that seduction, and because he died while the story was still hot.

This heat may well be genuine. Besides the generic Kennedy fame, there is a resonance to any tale in which women are treated shabbily by a Kennedy -- though given their track record, the babysitter should count herself lucky she made it home alive.

And it would be unrealistic to deny the cultural chord struck when a young, handsome Kennedy is felled in his prime. This chord turned to a choir when the image of touch football was added; though I have to put "football on skis" at the same level of stupidity as "skeet shooting in the round."

Regardless, it is the case that the pre-statutory-rape Michael Kennedy was a man of ability and accomplishment, that his business successes and eleemosynary efforts would have made for a glowing eulogy, and perhaps even allowed him to slip by St. Peter unnoticed.

But they would never have gotten him on Larry King Live.

This is the only "big news" of the tragically dumb death of Michael Kennedy -- that in today's America, a lifetime of accomplishment is worth less than a moment of infamy. The Era of Accomplishment -- of Edison, Ford, Eisenhower and, yes, Kennedy (Joe Jr. and JFK, that is) -- has been utterly usurped by the Cult of Celebrity -- of Dianas, Oprahs, O.J.s and the oafferies of the current crop of second-rate Kennedys.

In the America of Bill Clinton, the coin of the realm is celebrity, period. News directors have no interest in the notion that one story is, in and of itself, important or trivial. These former newsmen are in the entertainment industry, and if 10 million overweight women in trailer parks will stay up late to watch Princess Di's hairdresser give Richard Simmons a perm, then Dan Rather better grab his comb because he'll be broadcasting live from Ye Olde Beauty Shoppe during sweeps week.

Successful businessmen who start churches in Africa, provide warm homes for the poor and raise money for AIDS patients are not news. Kennedys who abuse drugs and sleep with underage girls are. And on slow holiday weekends, they make the front page.

Thank God For Racism

March, 1998

"I read all these dead white men and I'm tired of it. I think there is so much racism in this country because we don't understand each other."
--San Francisco high school senior Duc Nim.

Thank God for racism.

Reading the papers, I once again see how much Americans count on racism, real or imagined, to solve life's little problems. From the endemic failure of our state-run school system to the personal failures of incompetent individuals, racism is the grease that keeps our society running...in place.

Take, for example, the recent front-page brouhaha in Allendale County, South Carolina.

Allendale County has the kind of school system that makes the old Soviet Union look efficient and market-friendly. Residents there are more likely to have dropped out of high school before finishing the ninth grade than in any other county in South Carolina. According to The State newspaper, "Allendale's students are performing so badly that the state recently declared the school district impaired. Last spring, when 33 of Allendale's brightest students took Advanced Placement exams to earn college credit for their high school work, not one passed."

Then came the onslaught of media coverage, reporting that Allendale County's school system is a racial powder keg with a burning fuse: A black school board member pulls a knife on one of his white counterparts; he is removed from office, which sparks protests from black residents. A white principal suspends a black student for leading a school assembly in the singing of the Black National Anthem; student walk-outs and accusations of racism force the principal to resign.

Thus we see the immense power of the insidious forces of racism in South Carolina: Racial tension drove a school board member and a principal out of their jobs in the Allendale school system at a time when the school's own lousy performance could not.

Years of academic failure and wasted resources were taken in stride by the folks of Allendale. No protests, no student marches, no shouts of "Hey, hey! Ho, ho! Why do our test scores blow?" But the minute a white principal punishes a black student for breaking the rules (school policy prohibits racially divisive symbols like the Confederate flag, the Black National Anthem, Strom Thurmond) and suddenly the community is mobilized for change.

The same is true across the state as well. South Carolina ranks at or near the bottom in every objective measure of education performance. When polled, voters rank education as the most important issue facing our state, four times more important than taxes or crime.

But our public discourse rarely gets past the issue of race. Racists, on the Left and Right, claim that our state does poorly because we have so many black students. It's a never-ending conflict, but who is the winner? Why, the idiots running the schools, of course!

Think about the teachers responsible for Allendale's 33 "advanced placement" students who couldn't pass a blood test. In a rational world, they would be out looking for work right now. But nobody is holding them responsible for the quality of their work. Instead, black parents blame illiterate students on the insidious effects of "The Man keeping us down," while white parents, both liberal and conservative, write off their black neighbors as uneducable.

The same thing is happening at the national level, too. The same week that American high school kids tied with Cyprus for last place in math and science testing, the San Francisco school board was debating what the Associated Press called "strict quotas for non-white reading by San Francisco's high school students." The current reading list, with all that Shakespeare and Twain and stuff, is full of infamous "dead white males."

The argument offered by self-proclaimed anti-racists is that the reason little Johnny (or Juan or Chen) can't understand Chaucer is because Chaucer was a white guy. If Chaucer had been the Queen Latifah of the Middle Ages, American kids would be the literacy leaders of the free world, not the last-place losers we are today.

Does any rational person take this argument seriously? Of course not. But by deflecting the discourse towards race, the school boards managing our terrible schools are off the hook. Oakland has Ebonics, San Fran has "attack the Man," and our kids have the reading skills of the Sri Lankan 4-H club. What would the NEA, the San Francisco school board and the S.C. education department do without racism?

By the way, the kids have figured this stuff out. One West Coast student who demanded Shakespeare be replaced by Shaquille O'Neil said: "I'll tell you what Chaucer means -- it means subtitles required."

Yep, that readin' and writin' stuff sure is hard!

The big joke in all of this is that racism serves precisely the same purposes for these kids once they escape our classrooms. In Allendale County, rednecks complain that the reason they are making $4.50 an hour shoveling manure is because affirmative action has taken all the good jobs -- not because they can't add past their fingers or read the joke section of Playboy without a tutor.

In the same county, a young black woman's plight -- traveling 80 miles a day to earn $5.75 an hour cleaning hotel rooms -- is blamed on racism, not on the fact that she dropped out of high school when she was 15 to have the first of two children out of wedlock.

If it weren't for racism, these people would have to hold themselves responsible for their lives. Without racism, our schools and teachers would be blamed for failing our students. Without racism, all of us, white and black, would face the prospect that we are leading the lives we deserve.

So, on behalf of every American, I say, "Thank God for racism!" The alternative is too horrible to imagine.

The Will of the People

April, 1998

"Forget the law. Forget the facts. The will of the people, Mr. Starr, the will of the people."--William Ginsberg, attorney for Monica Lewinsky.

LOS ANGELES, SUMMER, 2002 - Legal observers and movie industry watchers emitted gasps of surprise and sighs of relief today when Hollywood mega-star Leonardo DiCaprio walked out of his cell in the Los Angeles County Jail, a free man. News of the film star's release sparked a rally on Wall Street, led by Warner Brothers stock, which rose an astonishing 235 percent on news that the jailed teen idol would soon return to the set of the long-awaited sequel, *Titanic III: Voyage of the Terminator.*

A clearly relieved DiCaprio was greeted with hugs from co-stars Arnold Schwarzenegger and Kate Winslet as he left the Los Angeles County Courthouse where Judge Lance Ito (brought out of retirement for this high-profile case) had released him. Moments earlier, prosecutors had dropped the first-degree murder charges against him due to "a lack of public support for continued action."

"Your honor, the people have spoken. We will abide by their wishes," Los Angeles prosecutors told the judge, referring to recent polls indicating that nearly 73 percent of all Americans wanted the popular film star released regardless of his guilt or innocence.

The prosecutors' decision caught many legal experts off guard, given the seemingly overwhelming evidence pointing toward DiCaprio. The victim was Los Angeles film critic Kenneth Turan, whose caustic criticism of the still-unfinished *Titanic III* and its cast appeared in print the morning of his death. Evidence included the infamous "bloody ship," a cast-iron replica of the Titanic used to bludgeon Turan to death; videotape from parking lot surveillance cameras showing Mr. DiCaprio leaving the scene covered in what appeared to be blood; and DiCaprio's own confession to his new girlfriend, Madonna, which she repeated in sworn testimony (Madonna and DiCaprio were married soon after her affidavit was released in what some legal observers viewed as an attempt to prevent her from testifying against her new husband.)

Despite the evidence, however, prosecutors were reluctant from the beginning to prosecute this case. One investigator told Variety: "I have a 13-year-old daughter who won't even talk to me!"

"This is the vindication my client has been seeking," said DiCaprio's attorney, William Ginsberg. "We knew the American people would never sit back and let these mad-dog prosecutors hound a beloved figure like Mr. DiCaprio for years on end. Someone needed to tell these prosecutors to get a life. Don't they know that if shooting isn't finished this summer, the film will never make a release date in time for the Oscars?"

Reaction to the prosecutors' decision was split down ideological lines. Conservatives -- clearly shaken by their increasing unpopularity -- were relatively quiet. Former Republican vice presidential nominee Pat Buchanan denounced the action from his secret bunker somewhere in Utah: "There used to be something called the rule of law in this country. Now, these kids beat you to death and, if they can get a movie deal-they walk! DiCaprio -- what is he, anyway -- some kinda wop?"

DiCaprio supporters like Geraldo Rivera and Larry King called the decision a triumph for democracy. "Our investigation revealed that many of the Los Angeles police officers were wearing the same style of uniform as the officers in the O.J. Simpson case. One of them had even met Mark Furhman. This was a witch hunt from the beginning," Rivera said.

Some legal scholars have expressed concerns about the emerging legal theory of "popular nullification" first espoused by U.S. Senator Hillary Rodham (former wife of President Clinton) in a 2001 appearance before the U.S. Supreme Court. In that case, all direct evidence of obstruction of justice -- including taped conversations, documents and sworn testimony by more than a dozen witnesses -- was set aside by Congress after what Speaker of the House Mary Bono jokingly referred to as the "70 Percent Amendment to the Constitution -- when your approval ratings are that high, you can get away with murder. Hell, I'd kill someone for those numbers myself!"

DiCaprio carefully avoided any indication that he was gloating, expressing his condolences to the family of the movie critic "...if, in fact, Mr. Turan was actually killed" -- a veiled reference to the "vast anti-Hollywood conspiracy" theory floated by *Titanic III's* producer James Cameron in a recent appearance on the *Today* show. DiCaprio also shook hands with some of the thousands of teen-aged girls who held vigil outside the County Jail.

"You have proven that, while you may not understand what goes on in a courtroom, you can still influence it. I love you all!" DiCaprio told the gathered throng, several of whom were clubbed violently to prevent them from reaching the smiling star.

When asked if she was bothered by the fact that DiCaprio had possibly committed murder but would not even be required to appear before a jury, one fan told reporters, "I mean, like, you know, like, people die and stuff, right? I mean, like, are you going to ruin, like, his entire career just because he maybe made one mistake? I mean, like, who's going to make *Titanic IV?*"

"Some of the old-fashioned types may not like it, but the people run this country -- with or without the law," Ginsburg told attorneys as he lunched with his law partner, former U.S. President Bill Clinton, and the President's fiancée, Playmate model Bambi Thumper. "Nobody's perfect, and imperfect people can't expect everyone to play by the rules, even when they make the rules, right, Mr. President?"

Mr. Clinton declined comment.

Meanwhile, Mr. DiCaprio announced that he would "get back to the job the people freed me to do -- make another great, box-office smash of a movie that will make everybody feel better about themselves."

"And I bet we'll get pretty damn good reviews, too."

What Do Women Want?

March, 1998

"Clinton approval ratings among women have been in the high 60s and holding despite intense publicity about womanizing allegations"--Pew Research Center pollster Andrew Kohut.

This is what Susan B. Anthony marched for?

American women, who have only been voting for about 75 years, are by their own behavior casting doubt on the value of universal suffrage. After years of damaging, demeaning and now indisputable evidence that President Clinton is a shameless boor who couldn't keep his pants on in a nunnery, America's female voters remain his strongest supporters.

It could be that the President's policies -- defending partial-birth abortion, advocating school uniforms, restricting right turns on red lights -- are of such vital interest to women that they must forgive him any oafish action, no matter how vile. If you are one of these women, I have a simple request: Please burn your voter registration card immediately.

It is rare indeed to hear a woman base her defense of the President on his female-friendly accomplishments. This is because President Clinton has no accomplishments -- feminist or otherwise -- to champion. We all know the cost of the Clinton presidency: He has turned the office itself into a joke, corrupted the criminal justice system, shredded the rules of campaign financing, brought locker-room language to the nightly news and landed literally hundreds of people either in jail, in debt or in the unemployment line -- most of them his one-time friends.

Sure, we all know what the Clinton presidency costs. The question is, what did we get for our money? Did we use a coupon, and is it too late to return?

And if we're comparison shopping, ladies, what is it you want from this President that is worth the price of silence in the face of his shamelessness? What policy has he successfully championed, what liberty has he tirelessly defended that is worth the cost we all agree he has inflicted upon our nation?

There are none. His greatest achievements, balancing the budget and reforming welfare, were policies he tirelessly opposed and repeatedly vetoed until the Republicans won the Congress. President Clinton taking credit for the Contract With America is like the airport baggage handler announcing he has successfully landed the plane.

But women still view him as their best friend in public office, their knight in...well, if not shining armor, only slightly stained. This is one reason I, as a man, am so offended by women's stiff-kneed defense of President Cretin as a typical American male.

My God, what they must think of the rest of us?

And yet, whatever they think of us men, Clinton's female voters think even less of his women. Kate Michaelman, pro-abortion extreminatrix, actually said of Paula Jones: "It is unrealistic for anyone to think that groups like NARAL and other women's rights groups are going to jump on board when she (Jones) was being promoted and bankrolled by groups that hold extreme anti-women views."

In other words, President Clinton can fondle all the pro-lifers he wants.

Even more fascinating are the catty, class-related observations about Kathleen Willey coming from members of the American women's movement. Paula and Gennifer couldn't get a "poor dear" from their fellow females. Meanwhile University of Wisconsin political scientist Charles O. Jones noted that Kathleen Willey's status in politics and society "means that more attention is going to be paid to her. More women will pay attention for the combination of who she is and the nature of the act."

Once again, the message from the Left is clear: Bop all the Big Hair-types you want, Mr. President -- we'll make more!

Not that the well-bred Ms. Willey is getting a completely free ride from the sisterhood. I am amazed at the number of women who have commented that, because of her offer to bring the President chicken soup, she should have known that their "flirtatious" relationship would result in an aggressive session of federal frisking at the Oval Office.

There is a mentality among some of America's most intelligent women that it is incumbent upon every female who approaches the president to do so with a "whip-and-chair" mentality. The subtext of their attitudes is that unless you walk into the White House prepared to beat back the attacks of the First Fondler, you are asking for trouble.

No one will ever accuse American women in the late 20th century of not being "intellectually flexible." But ladies, are you really prepared to replace the "glass ceiling" with the "ass ceiling?" Do you truly believe that for low-income women to move up in the world, their slacks should come down?

The unbending support of American women for one of the most cretinous, shameless and personally destructive womanizers to enter the public arena raises legitimate suspicions among men, suspicions we have long harbored about the distaff double-standard. You whine and complain about us regular-Joe types, who forget birthdays, let dishes pile up in the sink and don't understand how you could possibly sit through *Titanic* the first time -- much less go back. To you, we are insensitive louts who just don't get it.

But at the same time, you welcome our pants-free President with open arms of understanding and compassion. As long as he "feels your pain," he's welcome to feel up everything else of yours along the way.

The typical husband glances at a passing thong and you blame him. Bill Clinton reaches into an employee's underwear and you blame *her*!

What DO women want? Only their president knows for sure.

95

Silver Linings

February, 1998

Consider the events of the day:

Grim-faced Republicans trod stoically beneath the dark cloud of rising presidential polls. Democrats laugh nervously at their victory over scandal, but hold their breath every time a newscaster uses the phrase "oral briefing." The media provide a spectacle of self-flagellation, whipping themselves for the public cynicism they have inspired.

And me? I am overcome by joy.

Washington is in turmoil, but I arise each morning with a spring in my step. Commentators wring their hands, but I pass the day with a whistle and a smile. The media ask "What hath Geraldo wrought?" but in the evening as I log off the Drudge Report and climb into bed, the news of the world lulls me into a peaceful slumber.

I, once imbued with social annoyance, find myself unusually sanguine: Even my kicks at the odd, passing cat are insincere.

It's not just the cynic's joy of having my lowest expectations for my fellow citizens confirmed beyond contradiction...though that is a nice bonus. No, I am enjoying the endorphin-like rush of having been dealt an inside straight when everyone at the table is bluffing, the thrill of victory one feels on a blind date when your escort reveals that she was once a sorority girl.

Everything's goin' my way.

We are at a unique confluence of political forces -- right and left, local and national -- which seem designed to convince the citizenry that government is run by and for buffoons, that laws are made to be broken by the same people who write them, and that perhaps, just *perhaps*, the best thing for our nation would be for good men to do nothing and let the idiots fend for themselves.

In a word: freedom -- the happy coincidence of a complete collapse of the government's moral and social authority. And as a card-carrying member of the libertarian wing of the GOP, I couldn't be happier.

Historically, the two blunt instruments governments have used to beat down individual liberty have been morality (people should not be allowed to be naughty) and security (if we leave you alone, you might hurt yourself). Because people are reluctant to publicly oppose morality and because they privately suspect that, in fact, they are too stupid to prosper on their own, the fight for freedom has almost always been a losing proposition.

Not anymore.

Today, in the glorious Clinton era, the notion of government-inspired morality seems as quaint as a "Just Say No" bumper sticker. The idea of President Clinton proposing an expansion of government based on our nation's "moral duty" is as unimaginable as a call by this President for a day of national chastity.

When a nation has such low regard for government and the people who run it -- even the ones they "approve of" (79 percent and climbing!) -- the masses are unlikely to give it new things to do. President Clinton's strategy of staying in office long after he has become a laughingstock is successfully demeaning the power of every elected office in the land.

And I say, "Hooray!" Newt Gingrich couldn't do this much damage to the federal government with an SCUD missile.

At the same time, how can a public that sets its moral bar low enough to accommodate President Limbo seriously demand the enforcement of laws against vice, such as drugs, prostitution or gambling? Can you explain to a high school civics class why it's OK for the president of the United States to pay off a 21-year-old for her "services" with a

$40,000 job at Revlon, but a crime for Joe Blow to pay her $40 for the same "job" performed in the back of his Buick?

President Clinton has single-handedly removed the government's moral authority on any public issue. Liberty wins round one. Meanwhile, back home in South Carolina, there is a sea change regarding the issue of security, of whether or not people should be allowed to be stupid without government interference.

Thanks to advocates of video poker, the answer is "yes!"

The quasi-legal video poker industry has exploded across my home state of South Carolina. With its popularity has come a rise in libertarian thinking. Rednecks who support capital punishment for flag burners and a constitutional prohibition against interracial marriage have suddenly discovered Ayn Rand. Elected officials have begun articulating the once-unspeakable sentiment that, if freedom allows some people to fall through the cracks and to their own doom, that is not sufficient reason to restrict it. Folks, for South Carolina, this is practically a revolution!

True, liquor by the drink is still illegal in the Palmetto State and some blue laws still linger, but the end is near. Once people in power announce their willingness to allow self-destructive behavior, the question quickly moves from "Should Bubba be in a bar Saturday night?" to "What right does the state have to keep him out?"

Events in Washington D.C. and Columbia, S.C. are together landing a one-two punch on the power of government. The fiercely partisan, win-at-all-costs defense of President Clinton is based on the assumption that government has no moral authority to maintain. The money-driven defense of video poker is premised on the belief that government has no hapless citizenry to protect.

The result is citizens who have begun to ask the question, "Then what is government for?" From the people who run said government, the answer comes ringing back, "To keep us in power! Now give us your money and go away!"

An open-eyed citizenry is bad news for the institutions of government, but good news for those of us who always believed that individual liberty was more important than these institutions to begin with.

As that great political theorist Mae West once said of marriage, "It's a great institution; I'm just not ready to be institutionalized."

Chapter 5

The Meaning Of the Word 'Is'

Dear Hil,

July, 1998

Dear Hil --

Left this note on the dining room table next to the latest report on child immunization rates from the Department of Health and Human Services. Figured you would see it there first -- plus I never feel comfortable leaving documents up in our room. Who knows when they'll reappear? Ha, ha!

I signed that card you picked out for Chelsea and had the new Secret Service guy drop it in the mail. At least, I told him to. These new guys Bruce Lindsey hired for me since that whole executive privilege thing came up, why, they're so hard of hearing, I can't tell if they know what I'm asking 'em to do half the time.

Oh, and don't bother having lunch brought in today. I'm going to be downstairs getting videotaped. No need to come down and watch -- it's just the usual testimony. You know, that old "truth, the whole truth, and nothing but" routine. Boy, isn't it lucky we both went to law school? That sure paid off for us -- with or without those Whitewater checks!

Just kidding. Anyway, I know you're busy taking the villages and raising the children right now, but there are a couple of things I need to let you know about before that out-of-control, right-wing nut job Starr shows up with his video cameras.

Baby, you and I know that those vicious Republicans will stop at nothing to destroy the political principles that I have stood for all of my life. Some ideals are too important to compromise, like opposing the balanced budg... I mean protecting the safety net of welfar... uh, like nationalizing health ca... Well, Hillary, I don't have to tell you how important these principles are.

That's why the orning you went on the *Today* show and stood up against the Vast Right-Wing Conspiracy was one of the proudest days of my life. I believe we turned a corner that morning, as a nation and as a couple. In a way, you and I have come to represent all of America.

Hillary, I believe you represent the idealistic desires of the American people to use government power to improve and direct the lives of everyday citizens by redistributing wealth, ensuring justice and ending undesirable behavior. Meanwhile, my presidency represents what the government actually does to people once it gets all that power.

And polls indicate that most people like it, especially women.

Because we represent so much to so many, our enemies are determined to tear us apart. But we've always come out OK when we stick together. It's like that time in college when you found me naked in the pool with those girls from the swim team. You immediately wanted to jump to conclusions, but I swear, baby, if I hadn't torn off my clothes and jumped in to help them, those two girls would not be alive to serve as senior staffers in the Commerce Department today.

I'll never forget how hurt I was when you left me and started dating that Poli-Sci major from Boston. I was crushed. But eventually we got back together, and history proves it was for the best. Without you, I would never have become the proud husband and father I am, and I seriously doubt that Poli-Sci grad would have made you America's greatest First Lady -- in fact, I don't think she's ever run for public office, has she?

The point is, we've got to stick together. In the next few days, you're going to hear a few things that might upset you. You might hear about some DNA samples on a cocktail dress. You might hear that I have slightly modified some of my testimony from that deposition in the Paula Jones case. You may hear something about games of "Princess Warrior and Thunder King" at a late-night Oval Office party... (No, wait! You haven't heard that! Just skip it -- it's nothing.)

Honey, I swear I can explain this whole Monica mess. Like the stains on that dress, for example. We all know that, when she stormed out of the White House because I would not give in to her feminine wiles, that Lewinsky woman went straight to the Pentagon. Well, if you're a buddy of Linda Tripp and you're part of the conspiracy, how hard would it be to get a sample of my "bodily essence" from that top secret file they keep on every president? (Didn't I tell you about that? Why, they've still got bucketfuls of the stuff from JFK. Some top-secret cloning project. Very X- Files.)

I know sometimes you're tempted to doubt me baby, but you've got to remember why we're sticking together in the face of these false charges. These lies have one purpose only: to bring down my presidency and, with it, its most important legacy, namely, the protection from future prosecution we both enjoy. (By the way, did you ever get the real paperwork from the commodities deal awhile back?)

Hillary, I'm prepared to stand with you, to trust you when you tell me that I am mistaken about your orders to "fire those lazy bastards" in the Travel Office. I believe you when you tell me that those papers in my bureau for two years weren't under subpoena. I am absolutely ready to testify that it was not you who sent that "useful galoot" Craig What's-His-Name to pick up every FBI file that wasn't nailed down.

I swear, honey -- I believe every word you say. All I'm asking is that you do the same.

Gotta run, baby!

Your Bill

P.S. -- There's some cold chicken in the ice box. Don't wait up!

Clinton For Dummies

July, 1998

The President of the United States just made the most amazing four-minute speech in American history, putting his final mark on the White House intern scandal. While political junkies and Sunday-talk-show geeks like me are wallowing happily in the bottomless swamp of Clinton commentary, those of you with actual lives have been giving MonicaMania the casual attention it deserves. Instead of tossing my two-cents worth into the endless stream of talking heads, I offer this primer on "The Speech" in the hope that you regular Joes and Josephines can discover the joy of writing your own intern sex jokes in the privacy of your own homes. --MG

THE SPEECH

Length of speech: *4 minutes, 5 seconds.*

Amount of time the President spent explaining his relationship with Monica Lewinsky: *1 minute, 40 seconds.*

Amount of time the President spent attacking Ken Starr: *2 minutes, 25 seconds.*

Amount of time since the scandal broke that the President and his agents have spent falsely attacking Monica Lewinsky, Linda Tripp and the Vast Right-Wing Conspiracy: *218 days.*

Purpose of The Speech: *To save his presidency by apologizing to the American people for denying -- under oath and also on television -- that he had sex with Monica Lewinsky.*

Number of times in the President's *apology* he actually used the words "apology" or "apologize": *None*

104

Clinton and Me

Number of times he used the word "sorry": *None.*

Number of times the President used the words "lied", "cheated" or "ashamed": *None, none and, are you kidding?*

What did the president actually apologize for*?: Good question. The closest statement to an apology was: "I know that my public comments and my silence about this matter gave a false impression. I misled people, including even my wife. I deeply regret that."*

Didn't he apologize for having sex with a 22-year-old intern in the Oval Office?: *Not exactly.*

OK, how many times did he admit to having sex with Monica?: *He didn't give a number, but Monica has testified if you include the time they sneaked into the Lincoln Bedroom for a quick "staff meeting..."*

No, I meant how many times in his speech did he mention their sexual relationship: *None.*

How many times did he use the word, "sex?": *None.*

So did he admit they had sex or didn't he? *He said "I did have a relationship with Ms. Lewinsky that was not appropriate. In fact, it was wrong." That's it.*

Well, a relationship that is "not appropriate" could mean anything. He could have been talking dirty to her like Clarence Thomas was doing or he could have been trying to get her signed up in some multi-level marketing program. How do we know that the President really had sex with Monica Lewinsky?: *This is "Clinton For Dummies," not "Complete and Utter Morons."*

How did the President look?: *Remarkably bruise-free given the fact that he spent most of the weekend with Hillary. Commentators described him as "wooden,"(Slate), "more defiant then contrite" (*Washington Post*) and "he's still got a nice butt!" (*Time *magazine's Nina Burleigh).*

Clinton and Me

The President's lawyer told reporters that the President testified "completely and truthfully" to the criminal grand jury before he gave The Speech. Is that right? *No. The President flatly refused to answer several questions, so he didn't testify completely. We will have to wait to find out about the "truthfully" part.*

But he must have told the truth! Surely this man, more than any other, has learned his lesson about lying. He would never lie again, right? *Actually, no. In fact, the President lied in his speech.*

What? He lied on TV Monday night? *'Fraid so.*

About what? *It's kind of complicated. When the President was accused of sexual harassment by Paula Jones, he was ordered by the Supreme Court to testify under oath. In this testimony, he was asked if he had sex with Monica Lewinsky. The court was using a definition of "sexual relations" that was explicit -- the stimulation of the genitalia, buttocks, inner thigh, etc. etc. Using that definition, the President said "No." He claimed he never had sexual relations with Monica. On TV Monday night, he said that while this testimony was "legally accurate, I did not volunteer information."*

How could his sworn statement be accurate when he has supposedly acknowledged that she was "hailing the little chief?" *Only if you believe his argument that while she may have been having sex with him, he wasn't having sex with her. You know: "Eatin' Ain't Cheatin'." Unless you agree with this statement, then the President is still lying.*

So what does that mean? *What it means is that the Ferrelly Brothers' presidency is still in trouble. Ken Starr is almost certain to recommend impeachment, there will be hearings, Monica will have to testify before Congress exactly how she got the Executive Emollient on her dress, and so on. In other words, The Speech didn't do any good at all.*

Wasn't there any good news? *Sure -- ABC went right back to Monday Night Football. At least somebody is keeping a sense of perspective.*

Vice and Its Victims

July, 1998

"The Republicans aren't serious about [teen smoking]. They don't propose real children's smoking reduction targets backed by strong penalties. And there are no significant restrictions on the ability of tobacco companies to market their deadly wares to kids." -- Democratic House leader Dick Gephardt, June 23.

All 10 committee Democrats opposed a bill making it a federal crime for anyone other than a girl's parent or guardian to evade laws in her home state that require parental consent or notification for an abortion by escorting the girl to a state that doesn't impose those requirements. -- AP, June 24

Larry was a loser. A 21-year-old dropout who drifted between jobs, he hung out with the few high schoolers he could find still listening to Mettalica. One of those outcast kids was Nancy, a 15-year-old whose strict parents would not let her listen to rock music at home. Nancy discovered Black Sabbath from her worldly friend Larry, then he taught her to smoke. Eventually, he taught her the secrets of amore.

"Oh, God, Larry -- I'm pregnant!" Nancy screamed at him one day. "You told me it couldn't happen if I was on top!"

"And you believed me?...Anyway, you'll just have to have an abortion. Uh, you got any money, baby?"

"An abortion? Oh, no Larry -- I've always been taught that was wrong. I mean, my mom would KILL me...and besides, Allison told me you have to have your parents' permission."

When Larry finally got the nerve to call Planned Parenthood (from a pay phone in case they traced the call), he was told "this is a parental consent state," and was asked if he would like to write a letter of protest to his congressman. Eventually he found the number for an abortion clinic in a neighboring state. He shoved a handful of quarters in the pay phone and made the long-distance call.

"No problem," he was told. Amazingly, Larry discovered that all Nancy had to do was show up with the money early one morning, and by that afternoon she would be done -- no questions asked.

"Is this a great country or what?" Larry said to himself as he took a hopeful poke into the change slot on the pay phone.

Between some day work Larry picked up at a warehouse loading dock and a little money Nancy had tucked away, it only took a week to raise the few hundred dollars for the "procedure." He and Nancy didn't talk much during that week. Once Nancy tried to talk to him about how he felt, whether he thought abortion was wrong or not, but he just mumbled something about "women ought to have rights" and then refused to talk about it.

One morning before her classes started, Larry's beat-up Firebird pulled up outside Nancy's high school and she jumped in. They drove a couple of hours, mostly in silence. Though it was interstate most of the way, Larry compulsively referred to a map he had carefully marked using directions he had been given by the clinic. When they reached the squat, gray building, Larry circled a few times scanning the parking lot for trouble. Inwardly, he was terrified that there would be some kind of protesters, with police and TV cameras on the scene. He was afraid that if a bunch of Christians started screaming "baby killer," Nancy might back out and he would be in big trouble. Fortunately, the parking lot was quiet.

He pulled up to the building, but on the opposite end from the clinic door. "I'll be back to pick you up around 4:00, OK?"

Nancy stared at him dumbly. "You mean... you mean, you aren't even going to go in? You're just going to drop me off and drive away?" She burst into tears.

Larry looked around nervously. He thought he saw a face peer out of a nearby window. He reached for a cigarette. He was out.

"Look, uh, I'm out of smokes. Let's get a pack and talk about it -- really. Uh, it'll be OK. Really."

Larry found a convenience store. He left the car running and went in, while Nancy sat in the front seat, her head leaning out of the open window. He bought a pack of Marlboros and walked outside. He tore open the pack and lit one, letting the soothing smoke fill his pounding chest.

Larry walked around the car and stood next to Nancy. She looked up, and suddenly he noticed how young she was. He did something he had seen in a movie. He put another cigarette in his mouth and lit it. Then he took it out and handed it to Nancy. She smiled weakly. Maybe everything would be OK.

"Freeze!" someone shouted, and Larry felt his cheek smash against the windshield. Nancy screamed.

"Don't move! Police!" came another shout. Suddenly they were surrounded by blue lights and uniforms.

"Oh my God, oh my God," Nancy cried. She looked at Larry whose face had been dragged off the windshield and was now being pressed against the hood of the car by a hefty police woman.

"Would you look at this?" the officer growled. "This scumbag is 21, and that girl, well," she glanced pityingly at Nancy, "what is she -- 14 or 15? It's disgusting."

"How did you know?" Larry gasped through clenched teeth.

"We've had this place staked out for weeks," another officer told him. "We knew you punks were sneaking across state lines trying to evade the law. Don't you know what you're doing to this girl? Don't you have any morals at all?"

"But the woman at the clinic said the abortion was legal..." Larry moaned.

"Abortion? Who said anything about abortion? We're talking about -- these!" The officer waved the pack of Marlboros dramatically in front of Nancy's face. "Be careful!" the police woman snapped. "That's evidence."

"Oh, you're right." The officer glared at Larry. "You disgust me. Driving an underage girl across state lines -- and without her parent's knowledge, I bet -- then buying her cigarettes. I hope they throw the book at you, you repulsive child-killer."

As they loaded Larry into a squad car and watched the tow truck drag away the Firebird ("We confiscate cars from tobacco dealers in this state!"), the police woman shook her head sadly. There sat Nancy, sobbing on the curb outside the convenience store. "Hey, Sarge -- what about her? Didn't he say she was going over to the clinic?"

The officer in charge thought for a moment. "Give her a ride over there and put her on a bus afterwards. After all, she's really the victim here."

If It's Broke, Don't Fix It

May, 1998

"Authorities originally wanted to pursue Jackson's case as a felony. The charges were downgraded because the paper clip did not inflict serious harm." --From an AP story on 17-year-old Clint Jackson who was arrested and jailed after using a rubber band to shoot a paper clip at a schoolmate.

One of the most difficult notions for Americans to grasp is the idea of the irremediable, the unfixable: those unpleasant conditions faced each day that are not solvable problems but rather eternal facts of life like stupidity, apathy, and professional wrestling. Americans are the ever-hopeful offspring of Theodore Roosevelt and Thomas Edison. We are confident that, if we just put our shoulders to the wheel, we can roll over any problems in our way.

This uniquely American trait showed itself last week when a renegade student shot up the school cafeteria in Springfield, OR. Kipland Kinkel's irrational violence at Springfield High inspired yet another round of hand-wringing and calls to action in our public schools. As the mayor of Springfield put it at a funeral for one of the victims, "For Ben's memory, and for his family, we simply must do something."

What that "something" is has not been determined. There have been a few calls from the usual suspects for more gun control, nicer videos, etc., etc., but nothing has engendered significant support. One personal observation: A sure way to reduce the amount of youth violence is to stop naming children "Kip Kinkel." Stick some unlucky teenager with a moniker like that and you might as well hand him a rifle and point him to the nearest clock tower.

Beyond that minor suggestion, I have nothing else to offer as a solution to the problem of teen violence other than swift prosecution and eternal vigilance. But this is unacceptable to many of my fellow Americans because neither of these actions will guarantee that other children won't be shot in the future. In fact, I would bet that they almost certainly will. But that is no reason to "do something."

When concerned Americans attempt to eliminate the eternal problem of children behaving badly, it is their custom to find solutions that stop children from behaving at all. A few examples:

We all want schools to be free of drugs, right? Well, in pursuing this laudable goal, schools have recently taken to suspending students for A) giving a classmate a Midol; B) giving a classmate a lemon drop; and C) refusing to take a drug test as a condition for attending a public school.

And we certainly want our children to spend their school day free from the fear of violence. But as a result, A) a fifth-grader who accidentally brought her mother's lunchbox to school instead of her own was expelled when her mom's small paring knife was found inside; B) a middle-school student who offered to use a small pen knife to cut a cake for his teacher was arrested and held by authorities.

Schools fighting "hate crimes" have A) had a group of honor students arrested and jailed for hand-producing a booklet with jokes insulting the high school principal, who is black; B) expelled an honors student from a Concorde, N.C. high school for having a small Confederate flag (along with 100 other stickers) on her bookbag, and C) suspended a 13-year-old in Kansas for three days when he drew a copy of the Confederate flag on a sheet of paper at the request of a classmate.

And, finally, schools are fighting "troubled youths" by having our friend Clint Jackson arrested and jailed for shooting a paper clip with a rubber band, and by having an Ohio boy serve 30 days in the slammer for letting the air out of the bus tires at his school.

In each one of these incidents, the punishments are perversely excessive compared to the so-called "crimes." I can understand a school wanting to teach that drawing booklets with racially offensive jokes is a bad thing to do, but so is trashing the First Amendment. And while every mother in America may be genetically predisposed to assume that a flying paper clip will eventually put somebody's eye out, until it does, should the shooter be thrown in the slammer?

C'mon, people, this is America. We didn't even make O.J. go to jail, for cryin' out loud. But we're sending little Johnny to the joint for having a slingshot?

I will concede that one way to keep children from saying things we don't like is to censor them. One way to prevent shootings would be to confiscate all guns. One way to prevent kids from disrupting class is to force them to wear uniforms and not allow them to express their opinions, even on a book bag. And I have no doubt that capital punishment for practical jokes will make April 1 a less disruptive day in our public schools.

Such actions would make America a tidier, quieter and more orderly place. But who would want to live there?

There is no benefit in ridiculously restrictive rules or in their mindless obedience. We certainly should be distressed by the youth violence we've seen, but we must not heighten these tragedies further with a tragic reduction in our freedom from which we might never recover.

What I suggest is a healthy dose of anger aimed at the sick children who have fired the shots, an insistence that they be punished severely, and the acknowledgment that, no matter how hard we try, sometimes people do bad things.

Talkin' the Talk

July, 1998

If you had told the old gang back in Pelion, S.C. that Horace King had an idea worth $15 million, we would have laughed ourselves silly. And yet, that's exactly what a jury just decided.

I speak from personal experience when I mention Horace "Exalted Cyclops" King, state leader of the KKK and a resident of the rural South Carolina community where I grew up. Two of his sons, Vernon and Alan, went to school with me, to little noticeable effect. We didn't pal around (they seemed uncomfortable with people who conjugated their own verbs) and I wouldn't recall them at all if it weren't for their family's extracurricular activity -- promoting Klan rallies.

Every so often, a white van with a loudspeaker on top and a Confederate flag on the side would cruise up and down our road inviting us to a "Big Pro-America Rally, To-Night! All white public invited." Later that evening as my family headed to Wednesday-night Bible study, we would spot the motley bunch in the woods, huddled around some tattered, burning totem while Horace King yelled at them. It looked like a ragged remnant from the Lost Tribe of the Great White Trash. Or a cast of extras from a Kevin Costner flick.

There is a perverse irony in the notion of an anti-intellectual buffoon like Horace King being prosecuted for his (for lack of a better word) "philosophy." It's as though President Clinton were indicted for excessive modesty. But that's exactly what happened.

Mr. King's $15 million idea is that white people are superior to black people, that black people are evil and that white people who associate with black people are (don't try spell-check on this one) "wiggers." In a civil trial brought against the Klan by a black church which had been set ablaze, the arsonists claimed they were driven to crime by the persuasive powers of Horace King and these racist ideas.

We can argue as to whether these ideas are persuasive, but we can all agree that, pathetic attempts at vocabulary-building aside, Mr. King's ideas are not original. No, they have been heard all too often before.

Indeed, is there any Southerner, white or black, who hasn't been exposed to the bizarre rationalizations of the Exalted Cyclops and his ilk?

Trust me: Horace King has never had a thought -- original or otherwise -- in that thick, red-neck skull of his. So why does he owe $15 million to the thought police? What is his crime, other than, perhaps, plagiarism?

Shouldn't we prosecute the person who originally taught Horace King the secret Klan handshake? Isn't whoever put the Klan philosophy in King's head the real culprit?

One problem: The person stupid enough to believe in the Klan is probably too stupid to think up his own ideas, too. He probably got it from someone else, who learned it from his daddy, etc., etc. If we follow the trail long enough, we'll end up prosecuting Nathan Bedford Forrest, who is very dead (and, we can only hope, very warm).

This is the problem with prosecuting ideas. They are so hard to pin down. The Clintonistas may view this as a personal failing of mine, but I'd be a lot more comfortable if we just prosecuted people for their actions and left their ideas alone.

Does that mean words can never be prosecuted? Of course not. Defamation and libel are still actionable, and it's still a crime to yell "library card" in a crowded Klan meeting. But is Horace King directly responsible for the behavior of others who are stupid enough to believe his uninformed rantings? It's one thing if he drove the two boys to the church and loaned them money for the gasoline. But if he just announced his hatred of black churches and his desire to see them burn, is that enough?

If you answer "Yes, fry the racist bums!" then you must also prosecute preachers who speak out against abortion clinics, black Congressmen who label their Republican counterparts "Nazis," and, of course, Al Gore, whose "hate-filled" tome *Earth in the Balance* graced the bookshelf of the deadly Unabomber. To fail to do so is to fail your own principles.

I am far less principled than the fine members of the jury in this church-burning case who have declared thoughts to be deeds and words to be actions. I would have taken the coward's way out by only holding people responsible for their own actions. I would have sided with those weak-willed "wiggers" who see the freedom to speak as more important than the ability to shut up morons like Horace King.

No, I do not have the courage of those jurors who feel confident in their ability to determine which ideas are good and which are bad and to use the power of the courts to punish people whose ideas are just too unpopular to be allowed. I also don't share their confidence that they will be able to defend themselves should their ideas become unpopular one day.

The price of their courageous attempt at thought control is $15 million, give or take a constitutional amendment or two. Personally, when it comes to judging the mental efforts of Horace King, I wouldn't give you, or his prosecutors, 15 cents.

The Yankees Are Coming!

June, 1998

My wife, whose bloodline runs a deep, South Carolina blue, owns a T-shirt which reads: "We Don't Care How The Hell You Do It Up North." This fashion choice from an otherwise demure flower of Dixie is but one more bit of evidence that, as Northerners have long suspected, southern gentility ends at the Mason-Dixon line.

Interestingly, while we Southerners may deny any interest in how Yankees get things done, we spend an awful lot of time and money to mimic them. Take bagels -- please.

Take them back up North or out West or wherever you brought them from. The one thing we do not need in the South is another white, flavorless breakfast starch. If I wanted to spend my mornings choking down lumps of tough, indigestible dough, I would ask my wife to make biscuits again.

Bagels are an example of distinctly northern dining, like a bowl of clam chowder in New England or a bullet in the skull in New York's Little Italy. But though they are about as southern as a subway token, travel around our state and in every strip mall, in every grocery store -- even in the hallowed southern aisles of the Winn Dixie -- you will find them: bagels.

And not just any bagels, either. Spreading like kudzu across South Carolina are shops like New York Bagel and their competitors, Big Apple Bagel -- which is likely to be around the corner from Manhattan Bagel.

I know that South Carolina is a popular retirement destination for you disillusioned Yankees fleeing the wrecked Rust Belt cities you helped destroy, but my God, people -- didn't you leave anything behind? The New York state of mind is seizing control of our entire economy, and I'm not just talking delis.

Here in South Carolina we've got New York City Pizza, New York Life Insurance (don't they need a lot more of this than we do?) and, of course, New York Carpet World. Without leaving our borders, I can buy a suit at New Yorker Men's Fashions, pick up a hot new frock for my favorite gal at the New York Boutique, get my hair done at New York Stylists and wile away the evening at Manhattan's Nite Life.

And if that's not enough, Charlestonians can go to something called New York Moods, where, I assume from the name, cheerful Southerners can get an up north attitudinal adjustment. I have even written them a new motto: "Turn Your Jethro Into A Jerk!"

I am more sensitive than most to this new War of Northern Aggression because I just spent a year in Westchester County, New York. I can tell you first-hand that there is still plenty of northern aggression to go around. Ask a waitress in a New York restaurant if they have grits, and you might as well take out your teeth, strap on your banjo and start squealing like a pig.

"Grits?" one particularly parochial hash slinger barked at me last summer. "Wazzamattawitchoo? Weahdoyootinkyouare, anyway? Weahyoofum? Hey, Joey! Dis guy wants ta know if we got grits!"

Well, I showed her. I hitched up my overalls, stuck my John Deere hat on my head and stomped my bare feet outta there.

Having lived on both sides of the Mason-Dixon line, I have noticed a strange double standard. When we Southerners travel to the North and ask the locals to accommodate our cultural tastes -- grits, barbecue, inbreeding -- they react with indignation. "Wazzamattawichoo? You people are weird!"

Conversely, when Northerners traveling in the South find their ethnic needs occasionally unmet, their response is: "Wazzamattawitchoo? You people are weird." No matter which direction you take, the blame winds up here in the South. And I believe we Southerners, beneath the weight of our regional inferiority complex, tacitly accept the blame.

Clinton and Me

Southerners are the ultimate Upper West Side wannabees. We're closet carpetbaggers who believe in our hearts that we should emulate our big-city betters, with no expectation that they will return the compliment.

Consider the list of self-described "New York" businesses here in the bosom of Beauregard country. We Southerners would drive past a sign down here reading "New York Style Sex Club (Visit the Marv Albert Room!)" and not blink an eye. But the entire time I lived in New York, I never saw a sign for "Carolina Carpetworld" or "Dixie Hair Styles." No "Palmetto Boutiques" or "South Carolina Moods" either.

And what's more, I didn't expect them. It seemed perfectly natural to me that New York tastes would be accommodated down South, but that southern tastes would disappear in northern climes.

Southern scholars like C. Vann Woodward and John Shelton Reed place the blame on our native obsequiousness which, they claim, is a result of our losing The War. (If you have to ask which war, please move back up North now.) Having lost our nation's only military intramural scrimmage, a Southerner's tendency is to defer to our northern neighbors.

Maybe. Another more pragmatic view was best expressed by my Uncle Teenyboy: "Damn, there's a lot of Yankees! And them Catholic ones breed like rabbits." In other words, the North's demographic advantage means that, over time, our unique southern culture is doomed.

Whatever the cause, I believe it is time for defenders of southern heritage to respond in kind. Southerners must be legally recognized as a minority group and extended special protections. The federal government should implement a quota system setting aside road construction funds to build mustard-based Bar-B-Q joints along New York expressways.

National Endowment of the Arts funds could be used to foist Charlie Daniels on unsuspecting New Yorkers. We could even ask the World

Trade Organization to impose a swap: For every bagel we eat, a Yankee has to eat a chitlin'.

That'll show 'em.

My wife and I were decrying the decline of the South over drinks just the other day. She was drinking a Manhattan, and I had ordered a Long Island Iced Tea. The name of the restaurant: Broadway at the Beach.

"Bartender!" I yelped. "Two mint juleps -- before it's too late!"

Don't Mess With My Toot-Toot

February, 1999

Hey, reader! Come here for a minute. You look like a reasonable, liberal-minded person. Let me ask you:

Don't you agree that the state government should have "broad discretion in passing laws to protect the public?" We all want to be safe, right?

So you probably also agree it should be within "the power of the Legislature to prohibit the sale and manufacture of products it deems harmful." Sure, it should.

And despite what the libertarian wackos might think, there is no "fundamental right to own an item" that threatens your neighbors. The government needs to protect us from people who might own something that could harm our community, don't you agree?

Then, congratulations! You've just been elected....Sex Toy Czar of the state of Alabama!

All of the quotes above came, not from anti-gun activists or the Drug Enforcement Agency, but from state officials battling to ban all battery-operated pleasures from belles of Alabama. The legislature of the Cotton State recently proposed a law banning the sale of "any device designed or marketed as useful primarily for the stimulation of human genital organs."

Apparently, in Alabama it is a crime to own Monica Lewinsky's head.

Personal entertainment appliances, marital aids, provocatively-shaped vegetables -- it may soon be a crime to sell any of these items in Alabama. The state, which argues such products are obscene, contends there is no fundamental right "to purchase a product to use in pursuit of having an orgasm." The sale or distribution of such items within the borders of the Bubba State would be a misdemeanor punishable by a $10,000 and up to one year in jail... where such devices are unnecessary thanks to the earnest attentions of your cellmates.

Not surprisingly, the law is being challenged by the ACLU, whose ranks have been swelling since the story broke. Unofficial estimates place more than 5,000 women joining just during deer season alone.

Actually, the ACLU is representing several businesswomen, including B.J. Bailey, who sells sexual aids and novelties at parties; and Sherri Williams, who owns Loving Enterprises Inc., a chain of "romance boutiques."

"[The legislature] set out to eliminate strip clubs, but along the way they snuck in sex toys," Williams said. "Not only did they take away your entertainment, but when they were done they also took away your right to entertain yourself."

Yep, and if PETA succeeds in banning cow-tipping, Friday nights in Alabama are gonna get pretty slow.

Now, we as Southerners are hardly surprised when our fellow Confederates do something really, really stupid like this. But we usually have the good sense to be humiliated.

Not in Alabama. The government is enthusiastically defending its law prohibiting unauthorized vibrations. The Attorney General's office points out that Georgia and Texas have similar laws on the books, but apparently the men of those two states are attending to their husbandly duties with sufficient zeal that there has not been a need for widespread legal action.

"This is really a case about the power of the Legislature to prohibit the sale and manufacture of products it deems harmful," says state Assistant Attorney General Courtney Tarver. Harmful? To whom? Who is harmed by the proper use of a vibrator? Are intimidated husbands, threatened by their wives' self-fulfillment, risking Viagra overdoses attempting to rise to this unfair bedroom challenge?

I ask you, which society is more at risk: One where women pass their days with a happy smile on their faces and faint buzzing in their bloomers, or a community of tense, frustrated hausfraus snapping at their husbands, and leering at the paperboy?

But on the core issue -- the state's power to control the sale and ownership of legal products -- Mr. Tarver is absolutely correct. If the state has the right to prevent the sale of guns or cigarettes or pork chops or malt liquor -- all of which are unpopular with somebody -- why can't the state try to prevent mechanical naughtiness by forlorn housewives?

Once you give the state the right to stop your neighbors from buying things that you don't like, the state can use that right any way it chooses. Remember that the next time you growl at some poor smoker or grimace at an unapologetic gun owner.

Meanwhile, I have a plan for our lovers of libido liberty in Alabama. I think I know how you can escape the reach of the puritan police.

First, remember that the statute does not prohibit the use of sexual devices or prohibit the acquisition of them as gifts from other states. Perhaps those of us in neighboring states should break the embargo and airlift a few thousand "magic fingers" to Alabama. Imagine the joy on women's faces as the devices float down on parachutes from the sky.

But the solution isn't a legal challenge or civil disobedience. It's marketing.

Ladies, can't ever find a "D" cell battery when you need one? And when you find them, are the batteries already dead? Not any more! Now you've got Michael Graham's Guaranteed Home Battery Tester And Carrying Case. The cylindrical, tubular and rubberized Carrying Case (in sizes from 5" to "Oh my God!") keeps all your "D" cells together and easy to find. And when you flick the switch of this handy device, the quiet vibrations of your "Battery Tester" tell you they're all fired up and ready to go!

Coming to Alabama's finest hardware stores! Batteries not included.

The Envelope, Please

January, 1999

From the Academy of Political Arts and Sciences come this year's nominations for "The Rascals," the Academy's highest honor for individual performances in America's national comedy of errors:

Best Actress: Hillary Rodham Clinton, *Vast Right-Wing Conspiracy*. Once type-cast as a tough-minded Thelma-and-Louise feminist icon, The Artist Formerly Known as Ms. Rodham re-created herself as the Tammy Wynette of the White House in this televised tour de farce. Though the script for *Vast Right-Wing Conspiracy* by Sydney Blumenthal (*Liar, Liar*) is about as thin as an intern's thong, Mrs. Clinton performed brilliantly, helped by Matt Lauer's (*NBC's Today Show*) solid work as a gullible media dupe.

Best Special Effects: Jim Carville, *Ken Starr: Mad-Dog Republican*. Jim Carville made his reputation as a legendary storyteller in 1992 with his production of *It's the Economy, Stupid*, using his spin to morph the once-invincible George Bush into a hapless political has-been. Carville returned this year with another astonishing feat of bayou magic, using his wizardry to mutate the rabbit-like Ken Starr into a grand-jury Godzilla who filled audiences with terror. It's the greatest special-effects feat since Michael Jackson had himself turned into a white guy!

Best Sound Recording: Linda Tripp, *Sister Act*. The technique was primitive and a Maryland grand jury is reviewing its legality, but no doubt about it: Linda Tripp is the Edison of scandalous sound recordings. No edits, no "expletive deleteds" -- just the painful sounds of puppy love and doggy style.

Best Editing: White House Defense Counsel, *Enumerated Body Parts*. During their command performance in the toughest 100-seat hall in the business (the U.S. Senate), President Clinton's attorneys displayed an oversized copy of the definition of sexual relations used in the long-running show *Just Kiss It* starring Paula Jones. Jones' fans will recall that this definition listed in detail the specific body parts in "sexual relations" and all appropriate stage directions. In a brilliant editing move, however, the President's lawyers deleted that discomfiting sentence and replaced it with the innocuous phrase "enumerated body parts." Now you know why they made more money this year than Arnold Schwarzenegger.

Best Costume: The Gap, *One Blue Dress*. Accents by Bill Clinton. One stain. Well placed. It's a winner!

Best Original Script: William Ginsberg, *Dumb and Dumber*. Intellectually speaking, William Ginsberg and Monica Lewinsky may be the Shaggy and Scooby of the Clinton scandals, but for memorable, original dialogue, no one can touch the Bumbling Attorney from Beverly Hills. Even if he hadn't screamed obscenities at TV cameras or fumbled the biggest case of his life, he would still have staked his claim to greatness with one brilliant line: "Forget the law, forget the facts. The will of the people." Look for those words on the marquis of a presidential library near you!

Best Script Based on Previously Published Material: William Jefferson Clinton, *Perjury II: The Wrath of Ken*. "It depends on what the meaning of the word 'is' is?" "It depends on what you mean by 'alone?'" It may be weak logic, but it's boffo box-office, Bill! Mr. Clinton has always had a fine hand for fiction, but his astonishingly elastic vocabulary and imaginative view of the facts were at their hair-splitting best during this appearance before a federal grand jury. Despite numerous direct statements of untruth, the President crafted a script that friendly reviewers have even labeled perjury-free!

Best Actor: Alan Dershowitz, *I Saved Hitler's Brain*. A seemingly tireless performer, Mr. Dershowitz used his ubiquitous appearances on the cable news circuit to defend President Clinton from the "evil, evil, genuine evil" of monsters like Rep. Bob Barr and Sen. Trent Lott. More recently, Mr. Dershowitz told a crowd at Yale that if given the chance, not only would he represent Adolf Hitler, "I would win!" So much for the battle against genuine evil. Clearly, Mr. Dershowitz's attacks on the president's enemies are an act. And what acting it is...

Clinton and Me

Best Stunts: William Jefferson Clinton, *How Bad Do You Need a Job, Mrs. Willey?* Though best known for his thoughtful, emotive performances, Bill Clinton showcased his physical abilities in his role opposite Kathleen Willey. His strong, physical presence -- as well as his aggressive handwork -- also added to his performance with Monica Lewinsky in the year's biggest box-office smash, *Titanic II: Monica Goes Down.* Another of Clinton's strongly physical performances, the previously unreleased *Jane Doe #5*, is still in the can at NBC News and not yet available for screening.

Best Supporting Actors/Actresses: *You!* Once dismissed as puritanical, judgmental and unsophisticated, you, the people of America, have stunned pundits and pollsters in your role as President Clinton's most valuable supporters. Without your complex (some would say contradictory) supporting work, the President would have been trapped in a two-dimensional role made up of the facts and the law -- neither of which are complimentary to Mr. Clinton. The ensemble supporting cast created a fanciful environment in which the characters who lied under oath were sympathetic (Clinton, Jordan, Blumenthal), while those who upheld the rule of law were villains (Starr, Tripp, Christopher Hitchens).

No doubt about it: Without your leaps of twisted logic ladies and gentlemen, this comedy would have closed as a tragedy last summer. Instead, your support has ensured that America's most popular farce will continue with only minor rewrites until January, 2001.

See you next year!

'Twas The Night Before Christmas

December, 1998

'Twas the Night Before
Christmas
and at the White House,
a nubile young intern
slipped out of her blouse.

While at that very moment
up at the North Pole
a discouraged Old Santa
was searching his soul.

"For two hundred years
I've made nonpartisan stops
at the hearth of the White House
for quick Christmas drops.

"For Lincoln, a hat rack;
for Teddy, a bear.
And JFK never had enough
clean underwear.

"But it's my job to bring gifts
to the nice, not the naughty.
And this President gropes
every unguarded body!

"What will they say when they
find out St. Nick
brought goodies to someone
who can't control his own...
administration?

"No gifts at this White House!"
St. Nicholas cried.
"Bill's been very naughty
and he must be denied!

"Besides, any goodies or
presents or turkeys to carve'll
just end up in the hands of that
bug-eyed James Carville!"

Then what to Santa's wondering
eyes should appear
but eight well-dressed lawyers
in Eskimo gear.

They spoke not a word,
but their card said it all:
"Robert Bennett and Associates,
Attorneys-At-Law."

"We traveled north from D.C.
in the deadest of winter
in hopes that you, Santa,
just might reconsider.

"Our client's not perfect.
He may have misled
a juror or two about
who slept in his bed.

"But why must you leave
all his gifts on your bench here,
when most Americans instead
would support Santa censure?

"You may run the North Pole--
but we have Zogby and Gallup
and in a head-to-head race,
old pal, you'd get walloped!"

Santa spoke not a word;
he didn't want to match wits
with a gang that included
Cochran and Dershowitz!

"Our client will do better,
we give you our word, and
urge you to wait until you
call Vernon Jordan.

"Why, Mr. Jordan just told us
that Revlon is looking
for a large, bearded man
who enjoys lots of home cooking!

"They'll pay you six figures
as a senior exec.
Why they've already sent you
this generous check!"

Santa was outraged--
"I cannot be bought!"
Bob Bennett looked gloomy
"Yes, that's what we thought."

"In that case," said Bennett
as he opened his valise,
"I wonder if Mrs. Claus
might like to see these?

"They're pictures of you, Santa,
dusted off from our shelves,
but tell me--where did you find
such attractive young elves?"

It was true! Santa groaned as he
flipped through the glossies
of St. Nick himself
drinking Martini & Rossi's

with a half-dozen elfettes
from the toymaker's shop, less
their proper attire--
The whole bunch was topless!

"But I'm no Bill Clinton!
I never perjured or lied.
I haven't scored a babe since
I last cruised with Henry Hyde!"

"Alright, Santa," said Bennett,
"let's cut to the chase:
You bring Bill his presents,
or we'll bring a case!

"We'll hit you with lawsuits,
with orders and writs and
the sworn testimony of
Donder and Blitzen."

Clinton and Me

Santa knew he was beaten.
His fight, it was through.
He slumped into his sleigh
and took off... for 1600
Pennsylvania Avenue.

As Bill snuck into bed
about four hours late,
he heard the faint sounds of
reindeer and thought,
"Man, my lawyers are great!"

But he didn't hear Santa exclaim
as the reindeer flew past:
"Have a happy White House Christmas...
And let's hope it's your last!"

Chapter 6

"A Vast, Right-Wing Conspiracy"

What'd I Say?

April, 1999

CHARLOTTE, N.C. (AP) -- A radio talk show host was fired for making an on-air joke about the Littleton, Colo., school shootings. Just hours after the shootings, host Michael Graham related witness descriptions of the incident. He said:

"They (the assailants) were targeting minorities and athletes -- which, the athletes part, (is) one minor benefit to this otherwise horrible story." He immediately followed with "No, I'm kidding."

WBT general manager Rick Jackson apologized April 21 for Graham's joke, which he said was the most reprehensible on-air comment he had heard in his seven years at the station.

In a statement, Graham said: "... Without thinking, I made a stupid, insensitive and indefensible remark. On every show, I preach that people should suffer the consequences of their own stupidity. That principle certainly applies to me."

* * *

In case you missed it in the local papers, or on the national wires, or on the Drudge Report, or on CNN (good grief!), yes, I'm the moron who shot off his smart mouth and got fired for making a crack about the shooting at Columbine High School.

Like our beloved president, when I do something stupid, I like it to be really, really big.

You can read the quote above and decide for yourself whether or not I deserved to be fired -- *again* -- for something I said. But as for me, I'm not complaining.

While I disagree with my former boss's view that my fateful words were "the most reprehensible on-air comment" made on his radio station in the last seven years (I can think of a dozen things I've said myself which were worse), I completely support his right to determine who does and does not belong on his radio station. I am a true believer in free-market capitalism, and I will be until the day my unemployment benefits run out.

Seriously, I've received quite a few supportive e-mails (mail@michaelgraham.com) and calls, and while I appreciate the personal kindness, the comments have a disturbing tone. They imply that I am the victim of an injustice. I couldn't disagree more.

What happened to me was the natural, foreseeable consequence of my own actions.

When the spineless weasels at South Carolina Educational Radio banned me from their airwaves in 1991, they were reacting quite rationally to my on-air comments. I'm the one who went on their air and said that a tough, new ethics law banning criminals from state government meant "there wouldn't be enough legislators left to convene a quorum." Sure, the folks at SCERN approved the script and edited the tape. But when the complaints came pouring in, the choice for these cowering toadies was either standing up for the principles of free speech and an independent press, or doing the bidding of the semi-literate mouth-breathers in the General Assembly who control their budget and wanted to see me dumped.

Folks, this is a no-brainer! If the people at SCERN (Spineless Cowards Early Retirement Network) were truly principled, independent journalists, they wouldn't be working for the government in the first place. I knew that at the time, but I insisted on sitting in front of the mic and telling the truth about South Carolina's state legislature.

Hey, I'm lucky I wasn't lynched!

Then in 1995, when the General Assembly passed a budget amendment firing me, specifically, from my media lackey job in the S.C. Secretary of State's office, this, too, made sense. The firing was, in part, a payback for comments made in these columns, articles which contained the kind of literary material always unpopular among state legislators: irony, sarcasm, multi-syllabic phrases...

In a sense, these politicians were honoring my work. How would I have felt if the people I wrote about ignored my writings each week? Would it be better for my column to just roll off of their polyester-clad backs like spiked punch at a lobbyist's reception?

Instead, I got exactly what I wanted. I wrote stuff down. They read it. They hated it. I won. Okay, I got fired, but technically that's a win -- unless you're one of the many credit companies waiting for next month's payment.

So when I was invited to become a radio talk host at WBT in 1998, I went there with the same ambitions with which I wrote these columns. I wanted people to be engaged by what I had to say. I wanted them to react. I wanted what I said on the radio to matter.

Why, then, would I start whining now that it does?

What I said about killing jocks -- on that day, at that time and on that station -- was stupid. I shouldn't have said it, but I did, and what I said mattered. I'm glad. Poor, but glad.

This is in direct contrast to the self-serving hypocrisy of the Howard Sterns and Marilyn Mansons of the world. Like the pathetic, teen-aged losers who worship them, the shock/jock/rock crowd cries out to be heard, to be seen, to be noticed. Stern, Manson, Rob Zombie, et. al., scream "Pay attention to me!" all day long.

But when they say or do something so stupid, vulgar or ridiculous that it gets the attention of a grown-up, Howard and Co. just blush, look down at their shoes, and say "Who, me? Why, no one really listens to me. My words are of no consequence at all. Nobody's paying attention, are they?"

That was the ruse Howard Stern tried to pull after wondering aloud (and on the air) why Columbine's Dylan Klebold and Eric Harris didn't rape their female victims before killing them. When the stunned people of Colorado lashed back at his lame attempt at humor, Stern, as usual, played possum -- albeit a particularly ugly, juvenile, self-aggrandizing, hypocritical one.

The premise of Howard Stern's show is that stupid people have more fun. As a fledging talk show host, I absolutely disagree. Stupid people don't have more fun; they just laugh at the same joke over and over again.

But whether they are morons or Mensa members, Stern's audience deserve better than a talk host who pretends his talking is mere idle chatter. Howard, if you honestly believe your words have no weight, then why do you keep talking?

Those of us who want to participate in the great, national conversation -- either as a writer, a talker or a rocker -- we are in it because we want our words and ideas to matter, to have impact. When they do and the consequences are acclaim, life is good. But when our words strike hard and the results are unpleasant, the desire to run away from those words is mere cowardice, nothing else.

Well, unlike Mr. Stern, I am no coward. OK, so I'm not a genius, either, as I demonstrated on April 20th. But when I say that there are worse things to lose than a job; trust me. I speak from experience.

Loco

May, 1999

In Loco Parentis: The legal theory that schools may act in the place of parents.

What does it take for a school kid to be a rebel these days?

Failing grades? No way!

Complete illiteracy? Nah, that just gets you on the varsity football team.

Caught with a pocketful of condoms? Are you kidding? Who do you think gave 'em the condoms in the first place?

For the rebellious teenager of today who really wants to get in trouble with the American public school system, I've got just the thing:

Free speech.

Forget sex, drugs and rock 'n roll. A handful of sentences tossed upon the Internet, a line drawing or two, and you'll be the first hellion in your class to get suspended, expelled -- even arrested!

Don't believe me?

Ask the 13-year-old Arizona boy given in-school detention for carrying an electronics magazine to school that contained advertisements for guns. When he added a penciled cartoon showing the school blowing up, the kid was actually arrested by local law enforcement.

Another teenager was recently escorted off his high school campus and to the nearest police station. His crime? Wearing black clothing.

Since the Columbine High School tragedy, the American Civil Liberties Union reports a tidal wave of panic at public schools, leaving in its wake the wrecked academic lives of ambushed students. Public school administrators, whose incompetence and pettiness are legendary, have been using the Colorado shooting to give themselves permission to behave stupidly, not to mention destructively, towards the students in their charge.

135

Take the case of 15-year-old Andrew Eisen, an honors student in Antioch, Illinois. After a suspicious poem (yes, that's right, a *poem*) was found in his locker, Eisen was taken to the police station, where he said he was fingerprinted and charged with disorderly conduct. He then spent a week in juvenile hall and faces expulsion for the remainder of this school year and all of the next.

Now, we can all agree that 15-year-olds writing unauthorized poetry should be discouraged -- it can lead to other harmful lifestyle choices, such as majoring in English -- but should a student be arrested for a poem? And if so, how can any student walk the halls with a Walkman tuned into Marilyn Manson or Coolio?

More disturbing is the case of 11 students from Brimfield, Ohio, a small town about 30 miles southeast of Cleveland. The students had a Web site filled with images of dragons and castles and dark poetry, which had been created months before the Littleton shootings but was updated with comment on the massacre. The students called gunmen Eric Harris and Dylan Klebold fellow "freaks" and sarcastically praised them.

One statement read: "I wonder how long it'll be before we're not allowed to wear our trench coats anymore. You know those screwed-up kids in Colorado were wearing them, so that means I will also kill someone, and so will all my friends."

What's this? Teens using sarcasm? They must be stopped!

And, of course, they were. The school district's superintendent immediately suspended the students for the unauthorized use of humor and alleged independent thought.

However, the ACLU successfully fought their expulsion by arguing that schools have no right to punish kids for what they say off-campus. If schools have the right to monitor students' personal, off-campus Web sites, why shouldn't principals be allowed to read their diaries, too? Tap their phones? Eavesdrop on their conversations down at the Sonic?

The argument made by the anti-freedom thugs who run our schools is the typical Hillary-style hyperbole: "We've got to do something! The kid who writes provocative poetry today could be the clock tower shooter of tomorrow!"

But this is a false argument. The alternative to jack-boot justice is not helplessness and inaction, but rational action. What the hell is a school doing regulating any kid's off-campus speech? If schools want to ban trench coats and Rob Zombie CDs on school grounds, fine. If they want ban "threatening statements" on campus, no problem. (Pop quiz: What's the most threatening statement you can make to a public school administrator? "I support vouchers.")

But when some thuggish school administrator tries to destroy the academic future of a 17-year-old North Augusta, S.C. student for writing on his personal Web page that his ROTC teachers should "eat feces and die" (as was recently reported), the line of reason has been crossed.

Actions should have consequences, but not every mistake should be punishable with death. After all, we're talking about children. Is a police station really the best place to send smart-mouthed kids who need to learn a lesson in self-restraint?

Then again, if the alternative is leaving these children in the government-run school system, maybe we're doing them a favor.

Keeping Score

March, 1999

How stupid can you be and still attend college? It depends on how well you do on the boards.

No, not the college boards. *Back* boards.

Dennis Rodman I'm not, and the last year I played for the Pelion High Panthers, we won a whopping total of three games. So when I applied for college, I had to demonstrate that I could actually read and write, which meant doing well on the SAT. I got the test scores I needed and eventually went on to an illustrious collegiate career at a lousy, third-rate college: Oral Roberts University in Tulsa, Oklahoma. (Don't ask.)

Also attending ORU was a basketball star known around the campus as "Lester The Molester," a tribute to his high scoring record in a rumored one-on-one match-up with a reluctant cheerleader. Lester's SAT scores were comparable to my average points-per-game -- statistically speaking, non-existent -- but this did not prevent him from becoming a scholar-athlete in full standing. Or a starting forward for the ORU Titans.

Lester, an illiterate, anti-intellectual clod, had absolutely no interest in attending any university, no matter how low its academic standards. The Rev. Oral Roberts, no devotee of academic rigor himself (he did not allow his biology majors to study the theory of evolution) did his best to dumb down the university experience, but he could never drop standards low enough to accommodate Lester's limited intellect.

Why was Lester at ORU? To play ball... which is exactly what everyone -- teachers, administrators and the NCAA -- had to do to keep him there.

The bizarre dance between Lester the Molester and the ORU Holy Rollers demonstrates the core fallacy in the current debate over SAT requirements for student athletes; namely, that these athletes are in any sense of the word "students."

The serious players at most NCAA Division I schools, the players that matter, are not scholar-athletes, as the NCAA insists. They are minor-league professionals, working their way toward their personal goals of reaching the majors. The schools are the equivalent of a farm system, exploiting these athletes to generate entertainment revenues while offering low wages and limited benefits.

There is a major PR effort to disguise the obvious, but the competent students know why individuals who think Isaac Newton invented the fruit-filled cookie are taking up space in our classrooms.

Sure, there are some true scholar-athletes, most of them in sports like Intramural Rugby or Greco-Roman Snowboarding. But they aren't the reason for the lawsuit that inspired a federal judge last week to order the NCAA to stop using SAT scores as part of the criteria for admitting football and basketball players into collegiate sports programs.

And let's be clear on one thing: The athletes are complete academic incompetents. We aren't talking about people who confuse "effect" with "affect" or misstate the value of pi by a digit. We're talking about clods who are repeatedly unable to achieve the NCAA-mandated score of 820 on the SAT...an exam that gives them 400 just for showing up.

It gets even worse. Because the SAT scores on a scale from 400-1600, there are 1200 possible points on the test. Scoring 820 means you only have to answer enough questions right to earn 420 of those points. In other words, to qualify as a NCAA linebacker, you have to know a whopping 35 percent of the material covered in a multiple-choice test!

It is hard to know who is served by the federal government's order to eliminate SAT requirements and allow still more idiots into college sports programs, other than the idiots themselves and the coaches who consume them for our entertainment. Some see it as a civil rights issue, because nearly every highly recruited student-athlete who can't get past the SAT requirement is black.

No one has explained to me how a binomial equation can be racist. But let's assume that the SAT is somehow biased against black students. OK, how much is the bias worth? 10 points? 50? 100 points in the worst-possible scenario?

These failing athletes aren't even in the ballpark. The argument that these jocks are potential Einsteins who are being held back by biased testing practices might hold water if they were missing the cut-off score by a few points. But the decision by Duke University (average SAT score =1300) to reject the application of Joe Jock (SAT score = shoe size) isn't an act of discrimination. It's an act of mercy.

Why subject these athletes to assured academic failure? Why force their fellow students who actually want an education -- and the teachers who serve them -- to waste precious time and resources on the utterly incompetent?

Forget federal lawsuits by activist lawyers on behalf of academic failures. Let me suggest to every student reading this a new course of legal action: Sue the schools that put these idiots into your classroom.

The next time you find yourself sitting in class, bored to tears while your professor explains to Arnold Athlete yet again that the French Revolution did not sing *1999*, pull out your cell phone and call your lawyer. The university's athletic policies are denying you the right to the quality education that you and the federal student loan corporation are paying good money for.

Sue the university, sue the coach, sue the athletic director and definitely sue the stupid student. (Hey, he could have a lucrative shoe contract one day!) Ask a judge to explain why the students who want to learn should be punished to accommodate students who don't.

Of course, any student who filed such a lawsuit would soon be beaten to a pulp, if not by the athletes themselves, almost certainly by fellow students who dream of seeing their team in the Final Four. Chances are, anyone who takes on the current college athletics/entertainment axis is going to get slapped around.

Right, Lester?

Dead Foreigners

March, 1999

Before we consider the Clinton administration's policies in Bosnia, a brief quiz:

A charismatic, rabidly partisan political leader sends his troops to round up citizens, members of an unpopular ethnic minority, and herd them by the thousands into camps. Their property is seized, and many are forced to flee to their homeland. Is it a war crime?

If so, the criminal is Franklin Delano Roosevelt. The people in the camps were all American citizens who happened to be of Japanese descent. The year was 1942.

"But, Michael, that was war," you say. To which I reply: Precisely. And during a war, one person's "ethnic cleansing" is another person's "fight for Democracy."

The issue is war. And the reason so many of us here in America are having trouble getting a handle on the Kosovo story is that we completely missed Chapter 1: There Was This War...

The things people do in wars are nasty, brutal and hideous to watch. For example, what would you say if I told you that, in Vietnam, American soldiers shot hungry, nearly naked children, some as young as 10? Your reaction: "Those soldiers were animals! Lynch' em!"

But what if I then told you that these same children were carrying grenades and were about to dump them into our soldiers' laps? These soldiers are still child killers. But are they still animals?

Let's have another pop quiz: A nation elects a president who is wildly popular in the North, but so unpopular in the South that, despite the fact that his election was completely legal, southern partisans decide that the only way to preserve their culture is to secede. The supporters of the president, mostly in the North, find the South's way of life repugnant, and they also believe they have the right to uphold their democratic elections through force. When Southerners begin shooting and announce their intentions to leave the Republic, the North responds with violent, overwhelming force and preserves the Union.

Who is right? If you sided with the North and its battle to save the Republic -- congratulations! You've just joined the Serbian Army.

The "North" in this story is the Serbian majority in the northern portion of Yugoslavia. The South is the province of Kosovo, where the Kosovo Liberation Army (think the Confederate States of America converted to Islam) has been shooting police officers and duly appointed federal agents for years.

I'm not arguing that the Kosovo conflict is the American civil war, or that we should never get involved in intra-national conflicts, or any of the dozens of legitimate arguments that could be made by legitimately concerned citizens regarding our policy of blowing up busloads of Slavic civilians.

I am making the much more modest and obvious observation that the constant propaganda coming out of the Clinton Spin Machine is just that -- political pooge. It cannot be trusted.

Slobodan Milosevic is a pig, sure. But he is in a war, a war to capture territory. Unlike Saddam in Iraq, Slobo is fighting for territory within his nation's own borders. He was elected, in fact, because of his pledge to forever keep Kosovo part of his republic, to defend this mythic, ancestral home of the Serbs.

Milosevic is fighting this war, not against caravans of children, but against a real army -- an army so real, in fact, that just last year our own U.S. State Department declared the KLA a terrorist organization. The KLA is well known for running drugs and using prostitution to buy guns for their war for a "Greater Albania."

So why are we so outraged when people get shot and territory gets taken during a war? Because it's "ethnic cleansing?" May I remind you that American forces "cleansed" many an island in the Pacific of its Japanese populations not too long ago. By definition, taking territory in a war means getting rid of all the other people already there who want to keep it.

None of this is a defense of the Serbs. They are fighting a dirty, ugly war based on the notion that people should be grouped by their skin color and ethnicity. Unfortunately, they are being aided by the philosophies of our own Democratic National Committee -- who also advocate group rights and the over-valued importance of race.

But the Serbs are fighting an enemy who feel the same way. It's Greater Serbia vs. Greater Albania in a final battle to the death... the same battle they fought in 1389.

And into this mess we wander, led by the most inept foreign policy president since Jimmy Carter. We have chosen a side in this war, the terrorist KLA, and we are going to spend American lives and treasure to "liberate" Kosovo (or a big chunk of it, at least) from the popularly elected government of Yugoslavia and kill a few thousand Serb civilians along the way.

But keep in mind that the Albanians also claim parts of Greece, Montenegro and Macedonia, as well as Kosovo and southern Serbia. Now that President Clinton has made us their allies, what do we do when the KLA starts shooting cops in Athens? If the Greeks are smart enough not to shoot back, to just give in, to allow the ethnic Albanians in their country to secede, then I suppose we do nothing.

But if the Greeks defy the will of the American government, if they turn into "genocidal butchers" by actually defending their own territory, then we will be forced to bomb them into the Stone Age, too.

Alas, that is the price of American leadership, Clinton-style: lots of dead foreigners.

President Clarence

March, 1999

"Defenders of the president note that Broaddrick attended a political fund-raiser for Mr. Clinton just three months after the alleged rape." -- AP, 1999.

"Too often, targets of harassment are forced to defend their behavior. Instead of talking about what she did, what she wore, what she said, did she complain . . . we need to talk about why he abused the power that he had in this situation." -- Anita Hill, 1992.

Maybe Toni Morrison is right. Maybe Bill Clinton *is* America's first black president.

Since February of 1998, our Commander-In-Chief has been known in these pages as "President O.J." because we all knew what he did, we just wanted to see if he would get away with it.

And as Johnnie Cochran might say, "When the Senate acquitted, the name fitted."

Now that the President has been accused of raping a former friend and political supporter, the Clintonistas want to transform him from the O.J. of American politics into an updated version of America's *second* most resonant black political icon of the 1990s: Supreme Court Justice Clarence Thomas.

It's not quite a perfect fit, but it's close.

While both Clinton and Thomas grew up in poor, troubled families in the South, the similarities that leap out at me are largely political. Clarence Thomas was a weak candidate for the Supreme Court who was selected solely because George Bush needed a black nominee to replace Thurgood Marshall and Thomas was his best shot at winning a Senate confirmation.

Bill Clinton -- an unimpressive governor of a small state, a draft dodger with no foreign policy experience -- was a weak candidate for president, but his party needed a non-liberal nominee who wouldn't scare away every white, male voter in the U.S. The Left reluctantly accepted Bill Clinton as their best chance to win the White House.

Interestingly, they both survived scandals thanks to the weaknesses of their opponents and the unashamed partisanship of their supporters. Republicans like Arlen Specter and Orrin Hatch took on Anita Hill, and, while it wasn't pretty, they did convince 50 percent of American women that her story wasn't credible. Likewise, President Clinton's partisans happily trashed the reputations of Jones, Willey, Flowers, Lewinsky, et. al, to great effect.

In the end, one-third of the American people -- mostly white women -- loathed Clarence Thomas, but the Senate ducked its head and gave Judge Thomas the votes he needed. Less than a decade later, with one-third of America -- mostly white men -- screaming for his head, President Clinton was acquitted by many of those same senators.

And there is one other similarity between Clinton and Thomas that cannot be ignored: They were both lying.

Clarence Thomas almost certainly did some of the things Anita Hill charged him with. Then again, in the Clinton era, the charges now seem almost quaint: He hit on her at work, talked dirty, made a few off-color wisecracks. It's hard to believe that, way back in 1990, such behavior would put a man's job at risk.

In Clinton's America, Clarence Thomas' once-reprehensible behavior now represents the height of sexual propriety.

But Thomas ("I was a sexual harasser when harassin' wasn't cool!") denied every single charge: no pubic hair, no Long Dong Silver, no penile conversations. It was all part of the high-tech lynchin'.

And it is at this point that the similarities abruptly end. For polling at the time showed that most Americans believed Clarence Thomas' denial, while virtually no one today believes Bill Clinton.

Clinton and Me

President Clinton is the only public person in America whose denial of a crime is viewed as a confession. "Any allegation that the president assaulted Ms. Broaddrick more than 20 years ago is absolutely false," David Kendall, Clinton's attorney, said in a statement. And America hears, "I did not have sexual relations with that woman."

During his Senate confirmation hearings, 17 women who worked with Thomas appeared at a Capitol Hill news conference in a show of support for their former colleague. Nine took the microphone to say they had never seen, nor heard rumors of, any improper behavior on Judge Thomas' part. Not only have President Clinton's feminist allies been hiding under their beds as the Broaddrick story unfolds, but there probably aren't nine women in the entire country would claim they did not know of "any improper behavior" by our pants-free president.

Thus the key difference between President Clinton and Clarence Thomas is not the nature of their accusers but the nature of the accused. There was a perception, due in part to the presence of her liberal handlers, that Anita Hill might be lying to promote a partisan, political cause.

In the case of Bill Clinton, we have the reverse. Americans fear that his accusers, in pursuit of a partisan, political cause, might actually be telling the truth.

In honor of her largely uncorroborated, unproven accusations against a conservative Supreme Court nominee, Anita Hill was named "our Supreme Court justice" by Gloria Steinem. In honor of her corroborated, credible accusation of rape against the President of the United States, Juanita Broaddrick has been ignored by Gloria Steinem, Patricia Ireland and every other feminist/liberal leader in America.

What does this prove? That liberal supporters of the President are just as interested in justice today as they were when they called for Judge Thomas' rejection in 1990.

The similarities really are amazing.

Contempt!

April, 1999

Well, whaddaya know: Someone else finds President Clinton contemptible.

I cannot think of a better phrase to be forever linked to the Clinton presidency than the words "found in contempt," although "semen-stained" runs a close second.

Only, this is not just a matter of opinion. This is now a matter of law.

In February, the Clinton administration earned the distinction of being the first to have two of its Cabinet officials cited for contempt of court at the same time. Interior Secretary Bruce Babbitt and Treasury Secretary Robert Rubin were slapped with contempt citations for repeatedly failing to hand over documents related to trust funds.

At one point, a Clinton administration attorney said the reason these likely embarrassing documents couldn't be delivered was because they were stored in warehouses "infested with dangerous rodent droppings."

DATELINE -- Washington: "Rats Bring American Justice System To Standstill!" Yep, that's the Clintons, all right.

Speaking of rats, Susan McDougal also got out of her cage this week after spending two years in prison, in part for her dealings in the droppings-infested Arkansas banking system. Previously convicted of bank fraud, McDougal was acquitted of charges that she obstructed justice by refusing to testify whether or not the Clintons knew about her scams.

On the issue of contempt, the jury deadlocked, so Ms. McDougal is now free to appear five nights a week on Larry King and spew her semi-literate brand of paranoia and self-pity... and without an armed escort.

But there is one last tale to tell: In her trial, prosecutors showed McDougal a check for $5081.82 with a note in her handwriting that read "Payoff Clinton." This is a problem since a payoff from

Whitewater to Bill Clinton would be direct evidence of his involvement in the fraud. After foaming at the mouth and calling Ken Starr a minion of Satan, Susan McDougal explained that this check was not a payoff, no, no, no. It was part of a completely unrelated land transaction in *the town of Clinton*, Arkansas.

Oh, OK: Then what about the list of loans noting a person named "B. Clinton" and a sheet of interest calculations totaling up to the amount of -- you guessed it -- $5081.82.

This testimony, disregarded by a Little Rock jury that is itself under investigation, resonates with contempt: Contempt for the truth, contempt for the facts, contempt for the law.

Contempt has become one truly "distinguishing characteristic," as Paula Jones might say, of the Clinton era.

How appropriate, then, for the most self-righteous of politicians, the former law school professor himself, to be found in contempt by a federal judge. Judge Susan Webber Wright is from Arkansas; she knows the Clintons personally and is hardly a right-wing ideologue. How does she describe the president's behavior?

"Given the President's admission that he was misleading... and the clarity with which his falsehoods are revealed by record, there is no need to engage in extended analysis. Simply put, the President's testimony was intentionally false."

From a contempt standpoint, this is key. Remember that the President, his defenders and every lamebrain on CNN argued tirelessly that the President wasn't lying when he denied having sex with Monica and said he was never alone with her. He might have been misleading, but he did not intend to testify falsely.

To which Judge Wright responded, in the arcane, technical language of the law, "Yank, yank."

She notes in her order, "It appears that the president is asserting that Ms. Lewinsky could have been having sex with him while, at the same time, he was not having sex with her." Her head-shaking astonishment is the rational reaction to such an assertion. And yet the President gave us this nonsense for a year, aided and abetted by Lanny Davis, et. al., and a majority of right-thinking reporters happily accepted it.

This is the core of the contempt. The insult is not found in the act of serving us citizens this drivel day after day, but in the expectation that we will eat it.

Day after day, the White House sends out trays of indigestible nonsense: "We knew when we declared war the Serbs would kill all the Albanians... Why, we planned it that way!" or "Why would anyone tell *me* I was having coffee with a Communist Chinese agent -- I'm just the President!"

The Clintonistas contemptuously offer it to us as though we will accept it, as though we are so blind, so stupid, so forgetful that we will believe anything.

And that's when their poll numbers go up.

The only president in history to be cited for contempt, the only president who has been the subject of a credible charge of rape, the only president who we know has sexually harassed and shamelessly groped subordinate employees in the White House, the only president to have subpoenaed documents appear in his bedroom, to have built campaign databases out of his enemies' FBI files, to have changed public policy in a manner that allowed our enemies to arm themselves with nuclear weapons, who has taken millions of dollars from that same enemy to fund his campaign -- this is the president who today has the highest poll numbers in the history of a second-term president.

Contempt? You bet.

And if Bill Clinton feels contempt for the American people today, looking down upon us from atop his record-high poll numbers and record-low personal integrity, I'm certain it's for the same reason I do:

We've earned it.

Bad Boys, Bad Boys

June, 1999

The text of a hand-written note dated May 5th of this year:

Dear Susie,

I like you. Do you like me?

Please check one:

___ Yes ___ No ___Mabee

Love (?), Johnny.

PS -- I think you are the prettyist girl in the whole 4th grade!

* * *

The text of a letter dated June 15, 1999:

From: The offices of Cochran, Dershowitz and Hyatt, Attorneys-At-Law

To: Mr. John B. "Johnny" Smith, Jr.

Dear Mister Smith,

Pursuant to Title IX of the Education Amendments Act of 1972, as interpreted by the Supreme Court of the United States, John B. "Johnny" Smith, Jr. (henceforth referred as "Defendant") is hereby ordered and remanded to Cease And Desist all communications, conversations and interactions with Susan B. Anthony "Susie" Johnson (henceforth referred as "Plaintiff") until a thorough and complete investigation of the incident of alleged sexual harassment has been concluded.

Further note that Defendant is hereby under order not to destroy or tamper with any evidence which might be a relevant part of the investigation into your alleged actionable behavior. This covers all of written correspondence, including (but not limited to):

Love notes, book covers, tree-trunk carvings, bathroom graffiti (specifically those containing crude references rhyming with "France"); All notations in any form you have made using the "heart" symbol as a verb.

Defendant is also prohibited from discussing this matter further with classmates who may be called upon as witnesses. Any actions which may be viewed as attempts to modify or amend a classmate's truthful testimony -- such as offers of Pokemon toys or Star Wars: Episode One collectibles -- will be viewed as obstructing justice and could be punishable under the law.

Further, it is our duty to advise Defendant of the gravity of the charges which have been brought. Defendant's alleged behavior, if true, is in clear violation of Plaintiff's rights to a quality education, unencumbered by the oppressive atmosphere of sexual intimidation which Defendant created at Derwin L. Davis Elementary School.

While we are not seeking damages against the Defendant's family (we have completed our review of your father's tax returns through 1994), the $500,000,000 lawsuit which we have filed against Defendant's school district is a direct result of Defendant's alleged behavior. We believe that the court will find that it is the duty of our public schools to protect young women like Ms. Johnson from sexual predators like the Defendant.

We have read the testimony of your teacher, Ms. Brown, who claims that she was unaware of Defendant's behavior on the date alleged because, in her words, "I was too busy trying to teach these brats how to read to keep track of who was passing love notes." We find her comments, as well as Defendant's apparent lack of remorse, disturbing. We believe they indicate that Derwin L. Davis Elementary School is permeated with an atmosphere conducive to discrimination and harassment.

We would furthermore like to note for the record a preponderance of evidence that Defendant, joined by other students, engaged in discriminatory activity both on a regular basis and without interference from the school administration, including:

-- Games of kickball and tag which excluded female classmates.

-- False claims against female classmates that they were contaminated with a deadly contagious virus ("cooties") allegedly spread by casual contact.

-- Declaring the area within and immediately surrounding the monkey bars as a "Boys Only Clubhouse," and prohibiting female classmates from entering, a clear violation of the U.S. Constitution (See "U.S. v. Rotary").

In short, we find repeated incidents of harassment and discrimination by the Defendant which are actionable under the recent rulings by the Supreme Court. On behalf of our plaintiff, it is our duty to find those responsible for these actions so they may suffer the consequences.

We pursue this duty in defense, not just of the Constitution, but also the principles of individual freedom, and our right to a one-third contingency fee. We are absolutely confident that the negligible fiscal damage done to the school system by this lawsuit will be far outweighed by the benefit to students like Ms. Johnson who are struggling each day in a environment that denies them the ability to learn.

It is our hope that you will comply with the spirit and letter of this order.

Sincerely,

Cochran, Dershowitz and Hyatt.

P.S. -- We have also received reports that Defendant might know the identity of the student(s) who publicly accused you and Ms. Johnson of "sitting in a tree, K-I-S-S-I-N-G." You are therefore notified that you may be called as a witness in this case as well. Because you are white and Ms. Johnson is African-American, we are urging the federal judge to classify this case as a hate crime under appropriate state statutes.

Thank you for your prompt attention.

Curse of the Kennedys

July, 1999

The sudden, tragic death of John F. Kennedy Jr. is a true mathematical anomaly: Of all the Kennedys out there whose deaths would be a net plus for our republic, how did the grim reaper manage to snag the one decent apple in the barrel?

When I heard about JFK Jr.'s death, my first thought was "And that bastard uncle of his has a liver the size of a portable ice chest, but he's gonna live to be 100!" John-John's death added yet another piece to the growing evidence that Billy Joel was right: "Only the good die young."

I am genuinely sorry that JFK Jr. is dead. I was never a Kennedy groupie, but I was a *George* subscriber, and I had a casual admiration for a man who, though he could have turned his name and legacy of family tragedy into an easy ride for himself, instead chose to work as a prosecutor and publisher.

JFK Jr. hardly seemed aware that he was a Kennedy, and for that reason I was willing to forgive him for being one.

And it is an act of forgiveness. For despite all the talk about haunted families and frequent tragedy, it is not merely a curse to be a Kennedy. It is a genuine shame.

If there ever were a Kennedy curse, it was on the previous generation -- JFK, RFK and Joe Jr. When these three brothers, each endowed with great potential and ambition, died in service to their country (one at war, two by assassination), the generation of Americans who grew up with them were right to wonder why their best and brightest fell.

But not my generation.

JFK was killed before my first birthday. I have no recollection of his brother, Bobby. In fact, the first time I can recall hearing the word "Kennedy" was as a young boy watching the first moon landing on my grandmother's black-and-white TV in Conway, South Carolina. There was another news story that day about some guy named Teddy who had drowned his girlfriend while driving back from a party. The grown-ups watching the news with me were quick to point out that this Teddy guy was both drunk and married at the time.

For the rest of my lifetime it seemed, when they weren't killing themselves by shooting up heroin or slamming into trees playing ski-slope football, the Kennedys spent their spare time hitting on waitresses and playing "Spin The Bottle" with underage babysitters.

The current generation of Kennedys aren't our nation's princes. They are our punchlines.

This is hard for geezers like Dan Rather to understand. For people over 50, those who experienced Camelot, the Kennedy name still has some allure, some magic. When they hear JFK, they conjure images of glamour, of grace, of America's greatness.

But the Kennedys I grew up with aren't the Kennedys of Camelot. They're the Kennedys of Chappaquiddick. For my generation, the primary television image of a Kennedy isn't John-John saluting his father's coffin, but the hilarious *Saturday Night Live* sketches mocking "America's Royalty" in all their drunken, skirt-chasing, air-headed glory.

These are the Kennedys of today. Their politics are so out of date they seem lifted from one of the *Back to the Future* sequels. Their behavior is so self-destructive, every Kennedy male ought to be born with a warning label. Unlike the tragedies of the previous generation, these Kennedys are comic victims of their own weakness, irresponsibility and stupidity.

The sad victims in these Kennedy tragedies aren't great men brought low, but forgotten women undone: wives whose entire lives have been nullified by the Catholic Church, babysitters whose families are reluctant to bring charges, a young woman at the bottom of a lake whose death was not reported to authorities until after the politics were worked out.

And yet, out of this generation rose John Junior. Handsome, bright, ambitious -- we'd seen that before. But also relaxed, modest, untouched by the notion that America owed him its worship, dismissive of the idea that his family greatness overrode personal responsibility.

The talking heads (led, I am sorry to say, by my fellow conservatives) are pounding away at the "recklessness" of this inexperienced pilot flying into a dark and stormy night. They may be right, though I've talked to several pilots who agree that it was a close judgment call, one they had made before.

Regardless, I don't see any arrogance or outrageous behavior in Kennedy's decision to fly. No, the arrogance and outrageousness are coming from the media, as Rather, Brokaw et.al., struggle to revive the Kennedy family's hard-lost mystique using the loss of the son who had worked so hard to rise above his own name.

And talk about piling on: The media coverage of JFK Jr.'s death is filled with stories comparing him to Princess Di -- the People's Princess meets the American Prince. What an absolute insult to everything young JFK Jr. accomplished in his adult life.

To the tabloid American, John-John and Lady Di were two peas in a pod: attractive, wealthy and famous. How each of them got there is meaningless to the Great Unwashed who tuck them under their arm at the Food Lion counter each week and carry them back to their respective trailer parks.

But to lump JFK Jr. with Diana is as unfair as lumping him in with his own family.

Princess Di as a nobody who did nothing, a woman who found fame between the sheets of the men she slept with, and who used her fame to slip into the next, awaiting bed. She was all fame and no glory.

Meanwhile, John Jr. spent years working to achieve something of his own, something greater than the easy accomplishments that came from his unearned fame. He didn't hide from his father's name, but it wasn't his entire resume, either. He largely avoided the frivolous trappings of his fame, laughed at the undeserved acclaim and tried to build a real, resonant, grown-up's life of his own.

But he could not escape his legacy, not even in death. Thanks to our celebrity culture and *People* magazine mores, JFK Jr.'s accomplished life will soon be forgotten. Instead, John F. Kennedy Jr. will forever be linked to a horse-faced floozy from Buckingham Palace.

Now that's what I call a curse.

Discriminatory Practices

May, 1999

"We're not racists. We're snobs." -- Theresa Shackelford, lineal descendant of Thomas Jefferson and member of the Monticello Association.

When Theresa Shackelford publicly opposed allowing the unconfirmed descendants of Thomas Jefferson to join the elite Monticello Association, she reminded us all of the joy of discrimination.

As a tireless advocate of discrimination, I find myself constantly defending both the right and the need to discriminate, to discern differences, to sort people by their abilities and traits.

Note I said "sort people" and not "sort peoples." This group sorting, advocated by both David Duke and the Democratic Party, is what people generally confuse with discrimination. The two are not related in the least.

Racism is snobbery for stupid people. Trailer-park residents need someone to look down on, too, and racism allows those at the bottom of the social ladder to tell themselves, "I may be fat, stupid and poor, but at least I ain't no darkie!"

Unlike racism, which is anti-intellectual and involves self-delusion (i.e., the delusion that by demeaning others, you are somehow less of a loser), discrimination is dependent upon reason and self-knowledge. Discrimination is the ability to discern the differences between two people who *look* the same, but whose behavior or abilities makes them very different.

This is the style of discrimination practiced by Mother Nature herself.

After all, what is natural selection other than discrimination at the biological level? Was it fair that nature discriminated in favor of longer-necked giraffes, or against pea-brained simians? And while leopards don't chase gazelles out of any anti-gazelle bigotry, the food chain does discriminate mightily against the slow of hoof. We can have all the plant-eater encounter groups we want, we can try our best to build gazelle self-esteem, but the truth of the matter will never change: The slow ones get eaten and the fast ones don't.

This immutable truth of nature is currently creating a headache for Habitat for Humanity up in Charlotte, N.C. Habitat for Humanity is in the business of giving people homes, virtually for free. But in Charlotte, Habitat clients are in the process of losing their homes and returning to the streets. How, you may ask, do you get your home taken from you when it cost next to nothing and you are paying (literally) zero percent interest?

By going down to the local bank and taking out two, three or four mortgages on your new digs, and then blowing the cash on liquor and high living. One charity case, Julia Ann Addison, nearly lost her home after refinancing her $32,400 mortgage three times in eight months, sending her payments from $180 to $660 a month.

"This is not what I envisioned," said Addison, a single mother of three who openly admits her irresponsibility. Don't worry, Julia Ann. Neither did the liberals who bought you your house.

It's not easy staying poor amid the current economic boom rocking America. You have to work at it. The job market is so hot right now that there are anecdotal reports of American high school graduates getting jobs that *don't* involve a drive-thru window.

The dedicated poor, therefore, must repeatedly make stupid decisions in order to avoid prosperity. Otherwise, the trillions of dollars we've spent on social programs, combined with the red-hot economy lifting all boats, will drag these unfortunates into the mainstream against their will.

In 1995, there were 50,035 South Carolina families receiving cash assistance. As of April 1999, that number was 17,152. By definition, this remaining group is largely made up of incompetent clods actively clinging to poverty in the midst of plenty.

Well, what do you think happens when you indiscriminately give one of these morons a house? Do you think their lifetime of stupidity and irresponsibility are suddenly overcome by Ozzie and Harriet sensibilities?

Of course not! Instead, these geniuses start asking, "How many lottery tickets will you trade me for this three-bedroom ranch?"

Ah, but this is America, and so the rash of high-interest-rate refinancing among the Habitat dwellers is being blamed, not on the hapless homeowners, but on the evil mortgage companies. Local liberals are complaining that these businesses "take advantage of desperate or naive homeowners." These lenders are essentially making immoral loans, they argue, and they should stop.

Only one problem: Anti-discrimination (note that word) laws prevent banks from denying loans to anyone who qualifies for them. If a poor person living in a Habitat-built home were ever denied a mortgage for which they qualified, the bank would be prosecuted for violating equal-lending laws...prosecuted by the same Lefty-activists complaining about these loans.

Because we refuse to discriminate between the able and the incompetent, we've now made it possible for said incompetents to screw up their lives at a whole new level. I have no doubt that a few months from now, when these Habitat clients are both homeless *and* bankrupt, they'll thank us.

It is the inherent promise of Clintonism that more egalitarianism is on the way. One wonders if America's victims of non-discrimination will be able to survive it.

Who's For Jesus?

September, 1999

"They want to make sure that there are no more Jews!" -- Abraham
Foxman, national director of the Anti-Defamation League.

I cannot recall the exact chapter and verse, but I would urge my
Southern Baptist friends to heed this bit of gospel truth: No good deed
goes unpunished.

The Southern Baptist International Mission Board has published and
distributed a prayer guide for the month of September directing the
faithful to pray for Jews. The guide goes on to explain the Jewish high
holy days and give flattering portrayals of Jewish life around the world.

It sounds like the kind of innocuous, *Weekly Reader* religiosity typical
of our multi-cultural climate and which normally would pass unnoticed.
The problem: The Christians are praying for the Jews to convert.

And that ain't kosher.

At least, not according to Mark Briskman, Southwest regional director
for the Anti-Defamation League of B'nai B'rith. "We find this
offensive. It shows an element of arrogance because they are
specifically targeting Jews during this holy season."

Setting aside the propriety of Christians praying for Jewish salvation on
the eve of Yom Kippur, I am still trying to figure out why Jews would
be insulted by having someone pray that they go to heaven...which is,
after all, the purpose of the Baptists' exercise.

I don't want to shock any non-gentile readers, but Christian theology
condemns you (along with every Hindu, Muslim and liberal Democrat)
to burn forever in a lake of fire. From this viewpoint, Jesus' admonition
that "no one comes to the Father but by me" left little room for
negotiation. President Clinton himself would be hard pressed to wiggle
his way out of this one.

So I was taken aback when Abraham Foxman, national director of the Anti-Defamation League appeared on *CBS This Morning* shaking with righteous anger about the anti-Semitism he saw hidden in the Southern Baptists' agenda.

"They want to wipe us out through conversion," he railed. "They want to make sure there are no more Jews!"

Well, duh. Setting aside the oddball Jews for Jesus organization (Next: Hindus for Hamburgers!) the central tenet of Christianity is that everyone ought to become a Christian, just as Islam preaches the conversion of all infidels to the true religion of Mohammed.

Does this mean that Muslims want to destroy the Jewish race? Wait, let me rephrase the question...

Does evangelism equal anti-Semitism? I think not, and Mr. Foxman's own words revealed it. Part of his anti-Baptist ravings included reference to the fact that in the past, "Christians viewed Jews as not worthy of salvation."

Exactly, Mr. Foxman. If a Baptist missionary were knocking on doors in your neighborhood, but decided to skip your house when he heard the strains of "Hava Nagilah" wafting from the music room, that would be anti-Semitic. But attempting to share with you the gift of salvation -- which Baptists and other evangelicals consider a duty -- is the most embracing action a Christian can take.

Some Jews have complained that Christian theology itself is intolerant, that a religion that teaches everyone else is eternally damned is inherently hateful. Indeed, George W. Bush got clobbered with this not long ago, when a reporter asked him about his belief that "heaven is open only to those who accept Jesus Christ."

George W., being a politician of at least middling talents, backed away. "It is not the governor's role to decide who goes to heaven. I believe that God decides who goes to heaven, not George W. Bush."

But as Michael Kinsley of *Slate* magazine has pointed out, this is nonsense. If salvation is not mandatory, then George W.'s theology is meaningless. If Christ truly is "The Answer," then everyone who misses that question on the Big Final will spend eternity in a very warm detention hall, and George W. knows it.

So is it intolerant for a Christian to believe in Christianity? That is the question angry Jews are really pressing. Many Jews believe in God, but do not believe in heaven. A few believe in a heaven and a hell, and some hard-line Jews believe that gentiles have no soul ("nephesh") at all.

According to at least a billion people of faith on this planet, every Christian is doomed. And there are about a billion Christians who feel the same way about their fellow earthlings. Would this world be a better place if these two groups stopped praying for each other's immortal souls?

Perhaps it offends you to have people of other faiths keeping you in their prayers. But as my Jewish mother (deep down, aren't all mothers Jewish?) might say: "What can it hurt?"

Rev. Jesse Jackson, Where Are You?

November, 1999

"It's his home state, he'll have to come." -- Charleston, S.C.'s Elder James Johnson, on the Rev. Jesse Jackson

For the Reverend Jesse Jackson, it's a role straight from central casting:

A violent mob attacks two defenseless men as they bicycle down a dark road on the wrong side of town. The two are brutally beaten, one -- 35-year-old Troy Knapp -- with a lead pipe, leaving him in a coma. When the suspects are arrested, they claim their motive was robbery. The mob took two bicycles and insisted that the color of their victims played no role in their decision to attack. But the racial make-up of the mob indicates the victims were guilty of that classic Southern offense, "wrong place, wrong color."

A local church leader, Elder Johnson, has contacted the ACLU and other civil rights organizations with complaints of police improprieties in the case. He has also called on the Rev. Jackson to come back home to South Carolina and intervene.

But so far, no Jesse Jackson. Sixteen assailants charged with lynching, two men clubbed for the color of their skin, all back in Jackson's home state. Rev. Jesse Jackson, where are you?

Oh -- did I mention the victims were white? And their attackers were black?

And in one sentence, the mystery is solved. The media mob camped out in Jasper, Texas, and who followed the Rev. Jackson to Decatur, Ill., won't be headed to South Carolina.

The central problem with the Troy Knapp story is that the casting is all wrong. Ask the *New York Times* or CBS or any of the media outlets covering the Rev. Jackson's struggle for the Decatur 6, and they'll tell you the same thing: Sorry, Troy -- wrong color.

Imagine for a moment that the mob attacking Troy had been lily white - - say a roving band of Southern Baptists or Citadel cadets or delegates to the GOP National Convention. And imagine that Troy had been anything other than a white, heterosexual male. Care to guess how many hotel rooms it would take to accommodate the TV crews swarming into Charleston for that story?

Now, Decatur -- that's real news. White school board (well, 5-2, anyway) expels black students: Here's a story CNN can really work. OK, so three of the black "students" are third-year freshmen who had missed 350 days of school between them; and yes, they did beat the bejesus out of a bunch of bystanders at a football game, but still... they're *black*. Get it? Fight the power, take on the man, and roll tape, baby! I smell Pulitzer!

So does the Rev. Jackson, who got himself arrested to demonstrate his belief that these violent teen-agers should once again roam the halls of the same school they were flunking out of a few weeks earlier. As a cause celebre, these thugs may not seem like much, but the Rev. Jackson's keen sense of news judgment told him that, if he milked it, they (the networks) would come.

Not so for poor Troy Knapp. Black mob, white victim, blue collar -- somehow it's too, oh, I don't know, Rush Limbaugh for the American media.

The fact that this particular assault has not been declared a "hate crime" also blows the script. How is the Rev. Jackson supposed to explain that the three white cretins in Jasper, Texas, were racially motivated, but the violent mob of black bicycle thieves *wasn't?*

No, there is no leading man role in this story for the talented Mr. Jackson. However, Elder Johnson continues to hope that the good reverend might make a cameo appearance on the side of justice.

Oh, no, not on behalf of Troy Knapp. For the mob that bludgeoned him. The local minister is protesting the treatment of the assailants!

And, unsurprisingly, Elder Johnson assumes that Jesse Jackson will be on their side. After all, if the Rev. Jackson will take to the streets for the Decatur 6, whose criminal behavior was broadcast on national television, why wouldn't he champion the North Charleston 16, who had the foresight not to jump Troy Knapp in full view of a minicam? Aren't our local criminal losers just as good as that gang up in Illinois?

Sorry, Elder Johnson, but Jesse Jackson won't answer this casting call. This is a case of "Been There, Done That"... and not very well.

The reviews of the Rev. Jackson's performance in Decatur have not been strong ("Has Jackson simply lost his mind?" -- *Boston Herald*), and box office was hardly boffo. Jackson had to bus in protesters from St. Louis and Chicago to get a crowd.

Worse, the still-untold tale of Troy Knapp and the North Charleston 16 highlights the blatant racism that motivates the Rev. Jackson's character. In Decatur, he tried (unconvincingly) to play a complex figure who was looking beyond race and at the larger issue of zero-tolerance policies as a whole.

But what "larger issue" could the Rev. Jackson address by coming to South Carolina in defense of a racially motivated mob, even a black one? What story could he sell here, that as long as the Confederate flag flies on the State House, blacks are entitled to lynch a few "crackers?"

No, no, no. I suspect that when the Rev. Jackson is presented with this story of racial injustice, he will take his own advice and "Run, Jesse, run!"

Unfortunately for Troy Knapp – and the cause of justice -- the media will be right behind him.

Chapter 7

"One Of Our Greatest Presidents"

Bush League

August, 1999

Is George W.'s handling of the cocaine question Clintonesque?

While no Democrats are (quite) dumb enough to use this adjective, it is clearly what the White House lackeys have in mind as they push the cocaine controversy in the media. The Democrats are reading the same polls that I am, which show the Republicans with a whopping 40 percent lead over the Democrats on the question: "Which party can best protect the dignity of the presidency?"

President Clinton, whose white-trash mores and low-rent lasciviousness could undermine the dignity of an illegal cockfight, has demolished any hope that his party's nominee can be the standard-bearer for individual responsibility. As a result, the Democrats can only hope to even the score, to scorch the Republican's earth along with their own, to turn the 2000 presidential election into a choice between two evils.

Watching the same TV talking heads who defended President Clinton down to his last cigar suddenly discover, "Hey, waitaminute! Character does count!" is hilarious, but not particularly helpful. Their arguments indirectly comparing Bush to Clinton, which no journalist ever challenges, are pure nonsense.

And what has happened to the work ethic of the American media? Remember the good old days, when reporters actually used to... report? The deal was that the reporters would track down the hotel receipts and the envelope full of incriminating photos, print them on the front page of the tabloid, and then the candidate would break down at the press conference and announce that he was, in fact, in love with the llama and hoped his family would forgive him.

That's how it used to work: Reporters found out what really happened, and politicians tried to prove that it really didn't.

This has all disappeared in the press coverage of the Bush/cocaine question. Using the new Bush standard, there's no reason to do investigating. You simply ask a series of hypothetical questions, completely unsubstantiated by any facts or reportage, until you find one the candidate won't answer. Then you yell and scream until he does.

Edward R. Murrow would be proud.

So is George W. the ethical equivalent of Bill C.? Let's start with the most obvious difference between the two men, their accusers. In GWB's case, there are none.

Making unfounded allegations against your opponent to tie him up while you pick his electoral pocket is a well-worn and time-tested strategy in politics. The Clinton White House has played this game exceptionally well, but even for them the attack on George W. is a stretch because there is no actual accusation.

No one (as of this writing) has ever said, "I did drugs with George," or "George used to toke up in his dorm room," or "My God, he used to come to class with enough powder under his nose to start a ski lodge!" Not a single, solitary allegation of cocaine use by GWB has been made. Forget "guilty until proven innocent," W. hasn't even been charged.

Instead, the media are determined that he is going to convict himself by answering the question: "Have you now, or have you ever been, a regular listener to the Grateful Dead?"

Now compare W.'s list of accusers (nonexistent) to President Clinton's:

Clinton and Me

Juanita Broaddrick, Kathleen Willey, Paula Jones, Gennifer Flowers, Monica Lewinsky, Judge Susan Weber Wright, James McDougal, a dozen Arkansas state troopers and the entire Razorbacks cheerleading squad of 1990, etc., etc.

Get the point?

Thus far the Democrats have attempted to skip the "there is substantial evidence of wrongdoing" part (with the media's help, of course) and jump straight into the "Well, why not just answer the question?" stage. They are aided in this cause by W.'s GOP primary opponents who are desperate to slow down the Bush bandwagon.

Gary Bauer, an awful, little rat-faced git who has delusions of becoming the Republican nominee for president (or reliving the Spanish Inquisition, no one's really quite sure) has insisted that every candidate should answer any question regarding a felony.

Once again, journalism and due process are thrown out the window. Just sit down your candidate, get out your book of federal statutes and start on page one: "Have you ever...?"

"We ought to be able to say, with no hesitation, that no, we have not broken the drug laws of the United States," says Bauer. Then again, Bill Clinton used exactly that same phrase in 1992, and we later found out he was sucking a British bong in college, thus, the phrase "Clintonesque."

If, in 1992, Bill Clinton had said "None of your damn business," or "I made mistakes in my youth that I don't care to repeat," that would have been (for lack of a better term) Bush-esque. George W.'s answer to the drug question, which is designed to deflect, is very different from the President's, which, until he was caught, was designed to deceive.

In fact, George W.'s entire campaign thus far has been wildly different from the presidency of William Jefferson O.J. Clinton, and the "cocaine problem" is likely to highlight the gulf between the character of the two.

Will George W. be able to avoid the label "Clintonesque?"

By a nose.

Winning the Battle, Losing the War

February, 2000

"Bush is betting his ranch on a strategy of jihad [holy war]. Some of the telephone attacks are savage, portraying McCain as a hypocritical, temperamental insider who is soft on abortion, partial to Las Vegas gambling interests, in thrall to Big Labor and who has a budget plan that would cut donations to the nation's churches. 'It's not pretty, but it's going to work,' vowed one of Bush's top advisers." - Newsweek magazine, February, 2000

If you're a Republican who would like to be president of the United States, I have this piece of advice about the South Carolina Republican primary: Lose it.

Mock me if you will, but George Bush Sr. ignored me in 1992, as did Bob Dole four years ago, and you see where it got them: doing charity work and hawking Viagra. And this week, George W. Bush will make the same politically fatal mistake. He will win the battle for South Carolina and lose the war for the White House.

Yes, I am predicting a win for Governor Bush this Saturday in South Carolina, and since I'm already taking a ridiculously foolish risk (as I write, the election is five days away and the polls are too close to call), I'll go ahead and pick the spread, too: Bush by six. Or more. George W. is going to win because of his relentless, well-funded and effective attacks against the character and candidacy of John McCain. The Bushies have bought up every available minute of TV time in the state, they are bombarding local radio listeners with anti-McCain messages, and their paid phone banks are jamming the lines of wavering Republicans with comments about the Arizona senator that sound like they came from dialing 976-DIRT.

By driving down voter turnout and raising suspicions about a candidate who is already a bad fit for South Carolina Republicans, George W.'s go-negative strategy will give the governor an ugly win. What remains to be seen is whether or not this win will be so ugly that it keeps Bush from ever getting another date.

This has always been the problem with allowing South Carolina to play such a prominent role in the presidential nominating process. The things you have to do to win in this state doom you to defeat in the other 49.

Right now, for example, Governor Bush is running a barrage of ads and phone calls branding John McCain "soft on abortion." McCain's pro-life voting record is the same as that infamous liberal, Strom Thurmond. He wants to overturn Roe V. Wade, he wants abortion to be illegal in every state, but he wants to add an exception for cases of rape, incest and when the mother's life is at stake. And George W. thinks that's *soft?*

In the small, bizarre world of S.C. politics, John McCain's a liberal. In the rest of America, he's a pro-life extremist.

George W. is also attacking John McCain for being anti-tobacco, for backing campaign finance reform, even for encouraging independents and conservative Democrats to vote. In other words, the Bush argument is: "John McCain is an anti-tobacco political reformer whose position on abortion is the same as 80 percent of all Americans and who is popular with swing voters. We can't nominate HIM!"

Meanwhile, here is George W.'s list of "Things To Do To Win S.C. Primary":

✓ Kick off campaign at Bob Jones University, where interracial dating is prohibited and students are taught that Catholicism is a cult.

✓ Dodge all questions regarding the Confederate flag.

✓ Pick up endorsement of State Sen. Arthur Ravenel, who called the NAACP the "National Association of Retarded People," then apologized by saying he had unintentionally insulted all retarded people.

✓ Spend millions taking the most extreme possible position on abortion.

✓ Get televangelist Pat Robertson to act as your campaign spokesman on national TV shows the Sunday before the election.

Now, if you're running for president of the Independent Republic of South Carolina, that is, no doubt, a winning strategy. But outside the Confederate State of America...

In two short weeks, George W. Bush has managed to transform himself from the moderate-conservative GOP leader who would expand the reach of his party, and into the candidate of Bob Jones, Arthur Ravenel and Pat Robertson.

The thinking at Bush HQ is that beating John McCain this Saturday will knock the senator out of the race and allow Gov. Bush to move back to the center. But this is short-sighted because everything Bush has done has been captured on tape. It is a short-term strategy filled with long-term headaches.

Ask yourself: How many Catholics are there in swing states like Michigan and Illinois? How many moderate women in states like California and New York? How many rational human beings are there across the country, all of whom see Pat Robertson as the fringe loon played so well by Al Franken on *Saturday Night Live*?

Sure, in South Carolina, Bob Jones University is so mainstream that even the state's leading political reporter (Lee Bandy of *The State*) is a graduate. But in a one-hour interview, Tim Russert asked George W. at least five different questions about BJU and the bizarre theology it represents to people in mainstream America.

Which brings us to November, and Al Gore. Al Gore may not have invented the Internet, he may not be the star of *Love Story*, he may even have a bladder-control problem that keeps him out of important White House meetings.

172

But he ain't stupid.

All the videotape taken from South Carolina, all the strident, right-wing mail, the negative phone scripts, the resumes of the campaign supporters from our state — everything George Bush has used to win this race — will be used against him in the fall. It's all sitting at Gore headquarters right now, waiting for Jim Carville to pick through it.

So, to the Bushies on the eve of a South Carolina victory, I say: I hope you've got a lot of fond memories from here in Bush Country, because you'll be reliving them again this November—in Michigan, in California, in Ohio, and in living rooms all across the U.S. of A.

Barney Fife's Revenge

February, 2000

"Y'all go ahead and have your heart attack or stroke now. Have a good day."—Louisiana Sheriff's Deputy Bryan McClendon

If there is one element of modern American conservatism that completely befuddles me, it is my fellow right-wingers' affection for the police. As a true small-government conservative, I consider it my philosophical duty to dislike cops.

Not individually, mind you. Both of my mom's brothers are former law enforcement officers, and not only that, but (to paraphrase the Confederate flag crowd) some of my best friends are police officers.

Every day, there are many fine law enforcement professionals executing their duties with good judgment and common sense. Then there's the South Carolina Highway Patrol...

I'm kidding, of course. Picking on the South Carolina Highway Patrol is unfair, because doing so implies that other states' patrolmen — and they are almost *all* men — are not flat-topped Neanderthals with red-hot radar guns and unofficial quotas to meet.

Two recent stories sum up my personal experience with the highway patrol. The first is from South Carolina where state trooper Michael O'Donnell pulled over Sen. John McCain's campaign bus as it raced to some important GOP event. Did Trooper O'Donnell pull over the Straight Talk Express to (as the Bush campaign whispered) prevent Sen. McCain from personally performing an abortion on his own illegitimate daughter, whom he fathered with one of his Viet Cong collaborators?

No, Trooper McDonnell just wanted an autograph, and he didn't want to stand in line to get it. It was simply a star-struck state patrolman's version of a Blue Light Special.

Unfortunately for Trooper McDonnell, Sen. McCain wasn't on the bus he stopped and no real harm was done. However, the incident typifies the thinking that overtakes some members of law enforcement. It simply never occurs to them that there might be something they *can* do that they *shouldn't*. There's no inward analysis or questioning of the legitimacy or reasoning behind their actions, just that attitude that "If the good Lord didn't want me stopping you, he wouldn't have given me lights and a siren."

An even more egregious incident happened a few days later in Louisiana. A family, rushing a heart-attack victim to the hospital, was stopped by a deputy who made them wait while he wrote a ticket.

"Y'all go ahead and have your heart attack or stroke now. Have a good day," the officer allegedly told the driver.

The victim, Benjamin Basile, whose arrival at the hospital was delayed by half an hour, spent a week in intensive care. Not surprisingly, he was hopping mad...but not nearly as mad as he became when he heard that the local sheriff's office "has yet to determine if the officer actually did anything wrong."

OK, so what would it take for these badge-toting buffoons to figure out that having a heart-attack victim scrounging around for his license and registration is bad public policy? Would it take a death? Mr. Basile feverishly sucking oxygen from the officer's Breath-A-Lyzer in a desperate bid to stay alive?

My concern is not that police officers, like talk show hosts and writers, occasionally make mistakes. I'm worried about their unwillingness to acknowledge their mistakes and, worse, the attitude of the general public that the police are always right.

Quite frankly, this confidence in our law enforcement professionals has not been earned. We have more than enough reasons to view them, not with the benefit of the doubt, but with a dubious glance over their collective shoulders.

Right now in Los Angeles, 32 convictions have been overturned and many more cases are being reviewed because power-hungry officers planted evidence and framed people.

In Illinois, state executions have been postponed in the wake of the discovery that there were at least 12 men on death row who had not committed the crime that sent them there.

And in Charleston, S.C., the North Charleston Police Squad recently unleashed more than 30 bullets at an unarmed man sitting in his car, surrounded by police.

But there is no outcry. None of the officers involved in the outrageous shooting in Charleston, for example, have so much as been reprimanded, not even the officer who falsely accused the driver of having a gun. The police chief feels no need to dump a clearly dangerous officer because the community is thus far rallying to the department's defense. As long as citizens say, "They were shooting at a crook. He gets what he deserves," the cops will keep firing away.

Police work is a tough, grueling and often lonely job. I respect those officers who work hard to do it right. But I have nothing but fear and loathing for the authoritarian anal-retents who abuse their power.

And fear is the right word. After all, who polices the police? Out in L.A., it looks like the same officers who couldn't get the goods to convict O.J. are now planting enough evidence to convict *everyone else*. It seems that getting a special autograph or making their speeding-ticket quota is more important then protecting and serving the public.

The word I wish we could instill in these Barney Fife wannabees is "serve." There is no service in jerking around single girls going five miles over, or shaking down tourists who miss the 35-mph sign. Helping people get where they're going, treating them fairly and exercising some modicum of common sense, these are the most valuable assets our patrolmen have.

Or at least, I wish they had.

What About Bob?

March, 2000

"We love the practicing Catholic and earnestly desire to see him accept the Christ of the Cross, [and] leave the false system that has enslaved his soul"-From the new, LESS anti-Catholic BJU Web site entitled "The Truth About Bob Jones University."

Let me start with an easy question about the South Carolina intellectual-internment camp known as Bob Jones University: Yes, it is racist.

That this is even in question here in South Carolina shows how far adrift our state is from the continental United States, where BJU is viewed as a cross between *Hee Haw* and a bad episode of *In The Heat Of The Night*. Indeed, since the Bob Jones brouhaha erupted into the presidential primaries, I have repeatedly been told by my fellow South Carolinians that Bob Jones' ban on interracial dating is not racist.

I've heard the argument put many ways, but it is neatly summarized in FAQ format at www.bju.edu this way:

"Q: Is Bob Jones University guilty of racism because it has a rule restricting interracial dating? A: Students of all races attend here and live in racial harmony and respect for one another as Christians. Each person dates within his own race. For there to be discrimination, one race would have to be treated differently than the other."

This argument is, of course, a crock, the kind of poor pseudo-rationalization that passes for logic among the typical enrollee in a southern Bible college or school of straight chiropractic.

Bob Jones' ban on interracial dating is racist because it is a control of behavior based on race. The argument that no race is favored at BJU, or that black people don't want to date white people either, these do not make the policy any less race-based and, therefore, racist. What other word would you use to describe the segregation of people based on their skin color? Sexist? Ageist?

The premise of the interracial ban is that race matters, that race is somehow determinant, that people should be treated differently because of their skin color. This *is* racism, and the policies resulting from this world view are racist.

Now, you can argue that, using my definition of racism, affirmative action, hiring quotas and the like are racist. And you would be right. And, yes, it is true that many of the politicos currently attacking Bob Jones are die-hard supporters of race-based government policies that deny people jobs, quality education and even the right to vote based on their race. A few examples:

- In Mecklenburg County, N.C. last year, there were 1,000 empty desks in magnet schools and several thousand parents seeking admission to those same schools for their children. However, these children — white and black — were denied the education they sought because they were the "wrong color." Their admission would have made the schools too white/black for school-administered racial quotas. A law removing similar restrictions from S.C. charter schools has been opposed by some of BJU's most outspoken critics.

- In Florida, Gov. Jeb Bush has passed the "One Florida" measure, under which the state will stop taking into consideration race or sex when administering programs or accepting bids for state projects. One black legislator, who seized control of a state office in protest, insisted that ending racial quotas and treating all citizens the same would "divide the people of Florida based on race."

- The state of Hawaii turned Jim Crow on its head by denying white citizens the right to vote on certain offices dealing with programs for indigenous Hawaiians. The U.S. Supreme Court overturned the law last week, but the two judges voting to maintain racial voting restrictions were both liberals who support denying Bob Jones its tax-exempt status because of its treatment of people based on their ethnicity.

It's easy to see why George W. got confused about going to Bob Jones. When America views one form of racism as good and another as bad, it can be hard to keep score. Which is why those of us who want to get rid of the scorecards are so frustrated with Gov. Bush right now.

The fight by inner-city black parents for school vouchers, the success of Ward Connerly's assault on racial quotas in California and Florida, the collapse of support for race-based government favoritism in the polls, all these things were shaping up to help turn the 2000 election into a body blow to the Al "Sharpton" Gore view of America. There was an opportunity to use the upcoming election to fundamentally change America from a nation seeking to balance unfair treatment between groups to a nation where group membership simply does not matter. And it appeared that George W. Bush, with his "compassionate conservatism" and relative popularity in the Hispanic and black communities of Texas, might be ideally suited to deliver the knock-out punch against state-sponsored racism.

Then he got to South Carolina and succumbed to a seizure of redneck politics. It wasn't just kicking off his S.C. campaign at Bob Jones, or engineering the mailing of 250,000 pieces of pro-Confederate flag mail, or the attack phone calls from Pat Robertson, or the whispering campaign in Upstate churches about "Warren RUDE-man [sic] and the Jews in Columbia working with the liberal Jewish media to elect John McCain," or the "John McCain: The Fag Candidate" fliers handed out by over-the-top evangelicals in support of Bush.

No, it was the Bush campaign in toto that shaped the perception that George W. is willing to play ball with the worst elements in American politics if that's what it takes to get elected.

After two weeks of brutal press, George W. reversed himself and apologized to Cardinal O'Connor for going to BJU, calling it a "missed opportunity." Forget that. The real missed opportunity for the Republican nominee for president — and George W. Bush will be the

179

nominee — is the opportunity to overcome Al Gore and the politics of racial resentment with the principle of equal treatment under the law.

So much opportunity lost, just to win a primary in a rinky-dink state like South Carolina.

Who's Sorry Now?

March, 2000

"At Sunday's special Mass, the pope asked God's forgiveness for the sins of Catholics through the ages, including wrongs inflicted on Jews, women, and minorities."—AP

He may not be the most popular guy at Bob Jones University, but Pope John Paul II has a lesson to teach South Carolina: You can't have the heritage without the hate.

That, in brief, is why the Pontiff celebrated a special Mass repenting for sins committed by people long dead and asking forgiveness from victims long forgotten.

It is particularly ironic that we Southerners would receive this message from the Catholic Church, aka, "The Whore of Babylon." As a young evangelical growing up in a rural, South Carolina church, I was taught that not only were Catholics lost souls, but that they were mostly Yankees, which meant that they were condemned to spend their afterlife in New York.

Talk about eternal damnation...

Anyway, it's a good thing the Pope isn't southern. If he were, say, a member of the South Carolina General Assembly who supports flying the Confederate battle flag atop the state house, his Holiness would never have made such an apology. He would instead insist that he is the victim of rabid, Protestant bias in the news media, that the Inquisition wasn't about torture but about Church rights, that the Muslims who "converted" during the Crusades *liked* choosing between the cross or the blade.

And as a member of the one true and perfect Church of the Confederacy, the Pope would have avoided at all costs anything resembling remorse or responsibility for the lynchings, murders, assaults and riots that took place beneath — and in defense of — the Confederate flag.

Now, to be fair, for years the Roman Catholic Church did cling desperately to the altar of denial. Jesuit scholars printed millions of words in defense of anti-Semitism, the Inquisition and other historic misdeeds. And until recently, Catholic leaders would acknowledge no wrong-doing during the Holocaust, when the Church said little, and did even less, to prevent the horrors of Nazi Germany.

But apparently someone finally figured out, perhaps with divine intervention, that defending bad behavior was a poor use of time. Every scholarly dodge deflecting the Church's errors was a missed opportunity to celebrate its achievements.

And, compared to the Confederacy, the Roman Catholic Church has quite a record to celebrate: Preserving all of western civilization during the Dark Ages, inventing the university system, feeding the poor, caring for the sick, inventing bingo — there's a lot to brag about!

And, rightly so, modern Catholics celebrate their heritage of Michelangelo and Bach's Mass in B Minor as representative of their culture and a point of communal pride. But the Pope has made the Church's legacy even greater by acknowledging what seems self-evident to people beyond the Mason-Dixon line, namely that with the history of previous accomplishment comes the heritage of past shame.

Instead of picking and choosing their way through history, Catholic leaders are embracing something close to the truth. Detractors will always find one more sin to be acknowledged, one more wrong to be addressed, but the Church has achieved something great: It has strengthened its legacy of pride by acknowledging and embracing its failures.

Instead of the self-deluding circular arguments from flag-waving rednecks that keep history spinning into the present, the Catholic Church will, over time, put its failings behind it without losing its great history.

So why can't the Cult of the Confederistas follow this path? I talked to one die-hard Dixonian who said, "We can't have an institutional apology like the Catholic Church because the Confederate States aren't around. The Church has a leader and an organization. We don't. Who would apologize?"

That's a good point. But I have a suggestion for where to start. How about if every adult white Southerner over the age of 50 who wants to glory in the memory of the Lost Cause stand up and apologize today for Jim Crow?

How about if every person who says the Confederate flag is only a symbol of heritage, but who waved it in hate outside segregated schools and lunch counters in the 1960s and '70s issued their regrets? How about if every dew-eyed defender of Dixie fighting to stop Martin Luther King from having a state holiday declared a holiday on vindictive, personal attacks against their political opponents?

I believe there is an opportunity here, a path toward a positive resolution that could reclaim the legacy of courage and sacrifice of the Confederacy through accepting and acknowledging its sins. Unfortunately, that lesson we Southerners need so desperately to learn is being taught by the Pope in Rome, and I can already hear my fellow South Carolinians' response:

"We don't care how y'all do it up North."

Stop Making Census

April, 2000

To all households:

This is your official form for the United States Census 2000. It is used to count every person living in this house or apartment. Title 13 of the U.S. Code requires that you answer these questions. Please be as accurate and complete as you can in filling out your census form, and return it in the enclosed postage-paid envelope. Thank you.

Kenneth Prewitt

Director, Bureau of the Census

START HERE:

How many people were living or staying in this house, apartment or mobile home on April 1, 2000? Please print their names.

Person 1, Question 1: What is this person's name?

2. What is this person's sex?

Male___ Female ___

3. What is this person's age?

4. What is this person's date of birth? (NOTE: If questions three and four don't match, please request special simplified census form for residents of Alabama.)

5. Is this person Spanish/ Hispanic/Latino?

Yes, Mexican/Chicano ___

Yes, Puerto Rican ___

Yes, Cuban ____

No, just a plain old white person ____

5. What is this person's race?

White ____

Black, African Am., or Negro ____ American Indian or Alaskan native ____ (What tribe?)

Asian Indian ____ Chinese ____ Korean ____ Guamanian or Chammoro ____

Some other race ____ (Please list)

6. What is this person's ancestry or ethnic origin?

7. Is this person really sure he/she doesn't want to answer these questions? It is the law, you know.

8. Look, you can refuse to answer these questions if you want, but we know that you're an angry white guy who hates the government and has a stockpile of canned meats in your basement, so why not just go ahead and admit it?

9. OK, if that's the way you want it, fine, but just so you know, we're going to put you down as an African-American lesbian — and a single mom, too. Happy now?

10. That's better. Thank you for answering this important question, one that is vital to the efficient operation of your federal government. Now that we know you're a white male, just a few more, non-intrusive questions: How many guns do you have, and where are they?

11. Alright, pal. Let's include the ones under the bed this time, shall we?

12. Is this person a veteran of the military?

13. If so, how many times did you use the phrase "homo" while on active duty?

14. None? Yeah, right.

15. How much money did this person make last year from wages, salary, commissions and tips?

16. Sure, we already know. But the IRS asked us to double-check.

17. For whom did this person work?

18. Yes, we know that, too. Now we're checking on your boss. Hey, he's giving you the shaft, too, right? So feel free to jot down any incriminating information you've got on him while you're at it.

19. How many indoor toilets do you have? (If your answer is "Why, I'd never do that in my house!", please see previous note about obtaining special Alabama census form.)

20. State prisoners in Minnesota are currently being paid to fill out their census forms. How much would we have to pay you to get your full cooperation?

21. You are aware that if you refuse to answer voluntarily, you could BE one of those prisoners?

22. And finally, an essay question: Why do you have such a low opinion of your government? Why do you continue to distrust our motives and competence? What could we have possibly done to make you feel that way?

23. Wait. On second thought, don't answer that.

School Choice

March, 2000

What does it take to get an NEA member to support school choice? Why, just give the choice to the NEA!

That's the message coming from Hoke High School in Raeford, N.C., where the AP is reporting that three English teachers are "choosing" not to educate one of school's students. And the state of North Carolina says it's A-OK.

The ninth-grade student, Russell Almanza, was suspended for 10 days after writing an essay about a shooting at the high school. In the essay, Almanza portrayed himself as an FBI agent investigating the shooting. Like many novice writers, he used the names of people he knew, including his English teacher, Erica Johnson.

According to wire reports, Almanza said he didn't want to scare anyone. He claims that he wrote the story with himself as the main character who stops the violence and becomes the hero. "If they really read the story, they could see I'm the good guy," he said. "I never threatened anyone."

That may be why, upon appeal, the length of Almanza's suspension was cut in half. But it doesn't explain why, when Almanza showed back up at school, none of the ninth-grade English teachers would allow him in their classrooms.

As a result, this 15-year-old kid spends his English class period sitting alone in the school library. In fact, his teachers won't even send over his class assignments. His work is assigned and monitored by a teacher from another grade.

His mom says that Almanza comes home each day crying, complaining of being ostracized by the entire school over a single essay. And it does seem odd that a taxpayer-funded teacher in a taxpayer-funded school

187

has the ability to simply refuse to teach the child of a tax-paying family. Even those violent thugs up in Illinois that Jesse Jackson tried to help out were allowed to return to class eventually.

Nevertheless, young Mr. Almanza's banishment to the lonely library has the support of the Hoke High principal, the district superintendent and even the Attorney General of North Carolina, who has ruled that teachers have no legal obligation to educate children ... thereby decriminalizing the behavior of hundreds of thousands of incompetent public school employees across America!

The Attorney General's ruling is particularly fascinating for those of us who support school choice. Currently, it is a crime not to send your child to school. It is also a crime in most jurisdictions to sneak your child into a better public school by pretending he lives somewhere he really doesn't. Therefore, if little Mr. Almanza had tried to choose a different teacher by going to a different public school, he and his family would have been criminals.

But when he goes to the crummy school he's sentenced to by the school district and the teachers who are being paid to teach him refuse to, they aren't guilty of anything. Anything criminal, anyway.

What they are guilty of is hypocrisy. From the classroom to the Attorney General's Office, everyone involved in the case believes that this boy should not be in the school or the classroom he's been assigned. But they also oppose giving the kid's parents the right to pick out a different school or classroom, one where they believe he might get a better education. And so, young Mr. Almanza sits rotting away in the library every day, just the most blatant victim of the NEA's fear of freedom in education.

Why not let him leave? Where is the cry "Free at last, free at last!" rising from the library?

Because, as this and every other school district know so well, there are millions of other students who, if they could choose, would take the $7,000 or so we blow on each public school student and go buy a decent education from outside the bureaucratic bog. Teachers know this better than most people; that's why so many public school teachers have their own kids in private school.

The point of the story of Russell Almanza is that while opponents of school choice are quick to discuss the "cost" of school choice in dollars, they are loathe to admit the cost of the current corrupt system in lives. One life is being frittered away one untaught hour at a time in a school library.

There is another life, another story, that comes to mind: A 6-year-old girl killed by gunfire in a Michigan classroom — a classroom the girl sat in because she and her family were given no choice. She was shot by a classmate, a lost little boy living in tragic squalor.

My question to the administrators of Hoke High School, and every other opponent of choice is this: If the teacher of the 6-year-old shooter had wanted to keep that violent boy out of her classroom, should she have been given that choice?

If your good, liberal answer is "no," then why is Mr. Almanza sitting alone in a library right now? If your other good, liberal answer is "yes," then why do you deny that poor little girl's parents the same choice not to send her to that classroom to begin with?

Perhaps that would be a good term paper topic for Russell Almanza. He's certainly got plenty of time to work on it.

Somebody's Gonna Get Hurt

March, 2000

"It was an excellent concept, a great first step — I know that it will save the lives of many children in this nation."—New Orleans Mayor Marc Morial on the agreement by Smith & Wesson to make all new handguns "child-safe."

Two quick facts from the FBI about kids and guns:

✓ Number of children under 19 killed by gun accidents in 1999: 420.

✓ Number of children under 19 killed by guns *on purpose* in 1999: 2,216.

Consider this paradox: The more time we spend watching people shoot each other on TV and in movies for our entertainment, the less able we are to bear the violence that is an inevitable part of defending our freedom. Could it be that America is losing its bloodlust just when we need it most?

I began asking myself this question while watching two news stories break across each other on the great sea of CNN: Taiwan standing up to Communist China by electing a pro-independence party's candidate for president; and Smith & Wesson backing down from the soccer moms and their litigious allies in the Clinton administration.

Before you lapse into a coma at the mention of American foreign policy in Asia, please allow me just two quick sentences that may be relevant to you:

1. China could very well launch a military attack against Taiwan in the near future, an attack we have pledged to answer with American troops.

2. America probably won't, because our mommies won't let us.

Clinton and Me

As a loud-mouthed advocate of individual liberty, I am chest-thumpingly proud of our policy defending the democratic island-state of Taiwan from the Clinton/Gore Finance Committee (aka, "the Red Army.") During the Taiwanese elections, the more Chinese Premier Zhu Rongji rattled his saber about how the "Chinese people will use all their blood and even sacrifice their lives to defend the unity of the motherland" (sheesh, who writes this guy's stuff, Pat Buchanan?), the more I hoped Taiwan's voters would stick it in their eye.

But when Taiwan did just that, I gulped. "Hey, wait a minute," I thought. "This isn't some Tom Clancy novel. China really could decide to start WW III! And the last war with that many W's in its name involved drafting people *my* age!"

It's one thing to lay on my sofa and cheer the forces of freedom. It would be quite another to find myself climbing ropes at Fort Jackson and learning to say "I surrender!" in Mandarin Chinese.

More significantly, it would be a tough question for my nation. We've made a pledge to defend 22 million free people on an island 12,000 miles away. But if it came time for serious shooting, for Americans to kill and be killed in large numbers fulfilling that pledge, would we actually be willing as a nation to pay that price?

I doubt it. The last major test on that count was Vietnam, and even then we walked away from millions of citizens seeking democratic self-determination when the price got too high. What about Iraq, you ask? Grenada, Bosnia, Kosovo?

Exactly. As long as those wars were short, bloodless, TV-G affairs, we hung in. But the America which absorbed hundreds of thousands of casualties to defeat fascism in 1945 was not willing to bear even a dozen to stop ethnic cleansing in the Balkans just 50 years later.

Part of the problem is President William Jefferson Weasel, who lacks the moral authority to send a group of ROTC students into the girl's locker room, much less convince us as a nation that the blood of our sons must be spilled for an abstract principle. A guy who can't even keep his pants zipped for a good cause is inherently unable to talk me into getting shot for one.

But there is a more fundamental source of America's squeamishness over blood lost in the name of principle, and it's found in the other story I mentioned — the Smith & Wesson gun deal.

The Second Amendment to the U.S. Constitution has nothing to do with hunting Bambi or stuffing a Ladysmith in your handbag before heading to the parking garage. It has everything to do with the abstract principle that in a free society, no one entity — particularly the government —should have all the guns. The need to balance power between the federal government on one side and the states and their citizens on the other is the sole reason why the second-most important right expressed in our national creed is the right to keep and bear arms.

Like defending Taiwan, defending that right has a price, one which is all-too-often paid in real blood. One group paying that price are children killed in accidents involving guns. Their stories are always tragic, even more so for me since the day seven years ago when I became a father.

But let's put the tragedy into perspective. There are 280 million Americans, and a statistically insignificant 420 children died due to gun accidents last year. Reasonable gun safety measures make sense, as do reasonable controls on the production and distribution of guns.

But the reaction among soccer moms to this handful of deaths is to seize all guns, to put a slug right between the eyes of the Second Amendment. They don't want to hear about theoretical threats to our national security in an unforeseen future. They want to know that little Johnny is absolutely safe today, whatever the price.

Are these same women going to watch their husbands and sons die for the principle of democracy in a far-away land? Or are they going to, as some moms did during Bosnia, hold press conferences announcing that "My son only joined the Army to get a scholarship! I want Bill Clinton to tell him to put that gun down and come home!"

192

We live in a world in which democracy and freedom are always under threat and always will be. Defending these principles almost always involves real sacrifice today in hopes of a theoretical good tomorrow.

Rosie O'Donnell and Hillary Rodham are testing that resolve today. China and Taiwan may test it tomorrow.

When Bad Things Happen To Good People

April, 2000

When did my fellow conservatives forget the core premise of conservatism, namely that life sucks?

When it comes to the case of Elian Gonzalez, this obvious truth seems to have slipped away from once-solid conservatives like Brit Hume of *Fox News* and Rush Limbaugh, who of late sounds like Hillary slipped something into his Snapple.

In the old days, Rush was the first to seize liberal Pollyannas by the scruff of the neck and fling them onto the cold streets of reality. Now this formerly cold-hearted conservative is suddenly enamored of the idea that one little boy's happiness is both achievable and important to the future of our nation.

As L'affaire Elian unfolds, right-thinking conservatives are succumbing to the wrong-headed notion that principles should be abandoned when they become painful. This is absolutely contrary to the "no pain, no gain" philosophy that brought me to the conservative movement.

At the risk of committing a gargantuan simplification, the difference between liberals and conservatives is that liberals want to be nice, while conservatives want to be right. A bum wanders up to a liberal, and he gets a dollar because giving a bum a dollar seems like a nice thing to do, even if it buys said bum that one can of Sterno too many and he ends up in the county morgue.

Conservatives, on the other hand, reject the temptation (however weak) to hand over their hard-earned cash because doing what is nice encourages behavior that is self-destructive and wrong.

194

We know the bum might end up going hungry if we don't help. We further acknowledge that this might be the one guy in the world who would take that dollar, get himself a meal, get cleaned up and turn his life around. To which we reply, "So?"

The principles of individual responsibility and social justice (i.e., getting what one deserves) are more important than the misery of any one person. Indeed, we conservatives ask, what principle worth having *isn't?*

Defending the Second Amendment means some innocent people are going to be shot, you say? Fine, we answer.

Protecting free speech means some people will say hurtful, racist and stupid things? No problem, we reply.

And allowing parents to raise their children as they see fit means some will grow up in horrible homes exposed to bizarre, even dangerous attitudes like Christian Science, Pentecostalism and even Rotarianism?

Hey, that's life in the land of conservative principles. Or should I say, it used to be.

Conservatives used to believe in doing what is right and accepting the consequences. Now we believe in Elian.

I'm getting ideological whiplash watching President William Jefferson "Perjury" Clinton announce that "we must defend the rule of law," while his conservative opponents plead for us to look beyond the law and consider "the best interests" of the child.

What? Since when have we conservatives cared about the "best interests" of a specific child? Parading hard-case kids on TV to persuade America to throw the Constitution overboard is a tactic I expect from Hillary Rodham, not Henry Hyde.

And let me be clear: Unlike deluded Lefties and well-paid Commie stooges (like Greg Craig), I am perfectly willing to admit that if Elian goes home with his dad, his life is going to suck. Period.

And I have no doubt that life in communist Cuba is a series of daily tragedies for the millions who live there. Bad food, ugly clothes, long speeches and good cigars: That's life under a Cuban dictator.

But I don't care if Fidel Castro locks little Elian in a hotel meeting room with Tony Robbins and forces him into a lifetime of multilevel marketing. I'm not going to abandon the principle that parents should be able to raise their own children as they see fit, with or without the permission of the federal government.

Whether or not Elian lives in free-market prosperity or totalitarian squalor is not nearly as important as ensuring that all children from every country and every political system who are here in America are under the rule of law.

When Rush Limbaugh-types accuse me of not caring about Elian, I quickly concur. In the final analysis, I don't. Instead, I care about keeping an America where people raise their children with beliefs, behaviors and values their neighbors find objectionable, and nobody can do a damn thing about it.

I care about the ability of an American parent in Iran and an Iranian parent in America to know that their children belong with them, and that the American government will protect, not diminish, those rights.

Since the Elian case came up, I have been repeatedly asked "Would you have handed a child back over the Berlin Wall to a parent in Eastern Europe if the escaping parent had died?" My answer: Yes. And I know their lives would suck because of it. But by doing so, we would be protecting the values that make our nation a place people are willing to risk their lives to reach.

Protecting our principles, even when it hurts, is the right — and the right-wing — thing to do.

Mothers

May, 2000

"License and register all firearms. Ban handguns totally. They are made for one reason ... to kill people!" — *Rosie O'Donnell*

Watching chunky suburban moms hoofing their way along Pennsylvania Avenue in their comfortable shoes at last weekend's "Gunstock" festival, I realized why it took the Swiss so long to give women the vote. Motherhood does not make good democracy.

That's because mothers are always right. This was literally the primary argument made by the attendees of the media-friendly, Democrat-friendly, Gore-for-President-friendly "Million Mom March" in Washington. While many special-interest groups seem to think they know it all, this was the first group to openly declare so, waving placards reading "A Million Moms Can't Be Wrong," and "Guns. Bad. Now Go To Your Room" and (I kid you not) "Because I Said So."

How's *that* for a debating point, Senator?

There was plenty of attitude at the marching Momfest, as evidenced by the number of women using the phrase "pissed off." (Uh-oh, Mom's really mad now!) The mother of a Columbine shooting victim reminded us that "the hands that rock the cradle rule the world. ..You never, never tick off a mother." Then Rosie O'Donnell, the Sally Struthers of a new generation, glared through her insistently hip sunglasses. "The NRA buys votes with blood money," she says. "They are scary."

There was plenty of comedy, too, like the banner reading "When It Comes To Gun Safety, My Husband's an Idiot" (What? He can't work a trigger lock?) and a speech by one of the Kennedy clan in praise of Mothers Against Drunk Driving.

As they say at Chappaquiddick: Oops!

What was missing, alas, was math. Maybe the original talking Barbie was onto something with her observation "Math class is hard!" Maybe years of women practicing "whole math" on their ages and weights has taken its numerical toll. Whatever the case, the marching moms had real problems getting the numbers right.

First, not only were there not a million moms, but the organizer's reported figure of 750,000 marchers was greeted with audible snickers from every media outlet this side of *Mother Jones*. These exaggerations (What? Are you calling your mother a liar?) undermine the cause by raising questions about honesty and confirming the suspicion that the entire event was a Clinton-sponsored "Hillary For Senate" rally.

Secondly, the gun violence statistics spoon-fed us by the earnest, if uninformed, moms ranged from poorly interpreted to wildly incorrect.

For example, there's the oft-repeated statement that "4,000 children are shot to death every year in America." And this is true, so long as you include 19-year-old gun-toting, gang-banging criminals as "children." In fact, in 1997, the number of kids under 15 who died from guns was less than 600, about half of which were accidents and suicides.

Now, every death is a tragedy, and every death of a child is a newsworthy tragedy. But it is simply not the case that 600 deaths among 270 million people is reason enough to gut the Bill of Rights, no matter how much Mom cries.

Finally, there is one question that no one has yet been able to answer for me: How does refusing to defend your children from harm make you a better mom? These strident, Rosie-wannabes refuse to arm themselves and want to deny their neighbors that right, too. They are abdicating any responsibility for protecting their children from violence or threat of violence, and they are leaving their family's fate, should the worst happen, solely in the hands of the police.

Now, I understand that "Guns Are Nasty," as one marching mom's banner announced, and many women are uncomfortable around firearms. But is the bravest, most dedicated mom the one who orders her husband to get rid of Grandpa's old shotgun while she sends catty e-mails to Charlton Heston? Or is the best, bravest mom the one who overcomes her distaste for firearms and learns how to protect her family by unloading a 15-round clip in under 10 seconds?

Women seeking powerlessness, those co-dependent Clintonistas of the weekend rally, insist that owning guns merely makes things worse. "Guns in your home don't protect you. More often than not, they hurt or kill a loved one," Rosie insisted on a pre-MMM Internet posting.

Only one problem: It's not true. According to Florida State University research, people who use a firearm to resist crime are half as likely to be injured as those who offer no resistance. Criminologist Gary Kleck estimates that guns are used more than two million times a year to deter or prevent crime.

To me, the moms who learn to use guns, whether they are ever forced to use them or not, are heroes. They are defending both the Constitution and the more basic principle that parents must be responsible for the safety and well-being of their children.

As for that other bunch of mothers at Gunstock, take a little advice from *my* mom: "Just because everyone is doing it, doesn't make it right."

Rudy, Rudy, Rudy

May, 2000

"But Giuliani deserves credit for the kind of affairs he's evidently had. Unlike the predatory Bill Clinton, who riffled through vulnerable women like playing cards and demanded mechanical servicing from them like nameless plumbers, Giuliani has conducted authentic, long-term relationships with mature, intelligent, feisty career women." — *Camille Paglia, Salon magazine.*

"But as a woman and a wife, I can say that longstanding affairs with women who become constant companions are clearly more threatening to a marital partnership than cheap and transitory sex." — *Anna Quindlen, Newsweek magazine, the same day.*

Ladies, ladies, please: Make up your minds.

Here I am, your typical married man with small children. In other words, a eunuch.

Sure, I'd like to have sex. I'd love to have sex. I would *pay* to have sex which is why The Warden (my wife) never lets me out of the house with more than $5 and a Captain D's coupon.

However, I have also taken a vow of chastity in the presence of a clergyman. It began, as I recall, with the question "Do you take this woman to be your lawfully wedded wife?"

It is as a typical American married dad that I have been watching closely as typical American women debate the private naughtiness of their favorite public men. And I will confess: I am very, very confused.

When Monica Mania swept American womanhood in 1998, I could almost feel the ideological plates shifting beneath our continent. Women like Patricia Ireland, who demanded Clarence Thomas's head for allegedly talking dirty to an employee, launched a foaming-mouthed defense of President Clinton's career as a sexual predator. It took less than a year for these hypocritical harpies to transform NOW from a civil-rights organization into the National Organization for Whores, working the talk-show street corners for the Democratic Party.

But it wasn't just the NOW gang. More sensible women joined in the defense of President Corona and his policy regarding "face time" with nubile White House staffers. They might not agree with Mr. Clinton, who recently said that his years at the White House have been "good for my marriage," but many real-life women I know and usually respect found ways to let the president off the hook.

During Monicagate, seemingly normal, typical married women began insisting that infidelity was "no big deal," that "all men do it," that such behavior was to be expected. However, when I volunteered to join the teeming ranks of my fellow men and start chasing slow-moving receptionists around my office, my wife let me know that she had extremely different expectations for her husband than the rest of my species.

Observing this contradictory debate, I learned a lesson about women and politics: Ideology trumps morality, at least when it comes to men.

We are relearning this lesson with New York Mayor Rudy Giuliani. Writers like Anna Quindlen, a total Bill Clinton suck-up (pardon the pun), is not content to kick in Rudy's head regarding his infidelity. She also has to offer a defense of President Clinton's brand of adultery (high volume, low esteem) as preferred. To Mrs. Quindlen, Bill Clinton's habit of using the office help as sex toys is less troubling than Rudy Giuliani's seemingly long-term emotional involvement with career women.

It's Anna Quindlen's "Motel Six-Step Method To A Long And Happy Marriage."

By the way, Mrs. Quindlen's attack on Rudy Giuliani is entitled: "When Private Behavior Isn't" (answer: when it's under oath before a federal judge and grand jury), which is itself a contradiction to her writings during the impeachment imbroglio.

On the other end, politically speaking, is Camille Paglia, a tireless opponent of all things Clinton. In her column at the chick-friendly website, Salonmagazine.com, Paglia weighs in on the Rudy story and finds a way to take yet another kick at the First Philanderer. She argues that Giuliani's form of deceit is superior because it involves superior women. A roll in the hay at the No-Tel Motel is somehow shabbier than slipping into the coat closet with your executive vice president after a particularly steamy round of annual reports.

Watching these two fight, we married men are left scratching our heads, if not our seven-year itches.

It never occurred to us that the relationship between the married man and the sideline squeeze mattered. We — maybe it's just a naive "I" — assumed that it was the relationship between the husband and wife that was the issue. Violating that trust, with Monica Lewinsky or Margaret Thatcher, would seem to be an inherently bad thing.

When women articulate these more nuanced debates about which are the less-offensive forms of adultery, what their men hear is "Go get 'em, boys!" Give us an inch, and we'll take the entire data entry department.

There are always excuses for cheating. I just didn't think there were any that women would actually accept. This is a whole new world. After all, ladies, if you're looking for mitigating factors for philandering, Bill Clinton has the ultimate excuse for sleeping around — his *wife*. Being married to that tree-legged, tantrum-throwing, emasculating shrew puts a husband in the Jim Bakker class of cheaters as far as we men are concerned:

None of the rest of us would sleep with Mrs. Clinton, either.

So far, however, it appears that politics is the key. If your guy is naughty, it's an understandable mistake. If the other team's guy slips from the straight and narrow, hangin's too good for him.

And if the women of America are going to permit extramarital sex based on partisanship, all I've got to say is this: How can I get Anna Nicole Smith to join the Republican Party?

Ouch! Just kidding, honey.

The Million-Dollar Question

June, 2000

[Cue music. The camera pans as Regis enters stage left.]

REEGE: Good evening, everyone, and welcome to ABC's latest edition to America's game-show craze, "Who Wants to Be A Limousine Liberal?"

[Applause. Cue lights. Dramatic techno-pop version of "Happy Days Are Here Again" plays as Regis takes his place at the console.]

REEGE: Our first contestant tonight is a soccer mom from Irmo, South Carolina, Tara Barkwell! Welcome, Tara. Are you nervous?

TARA: A little, I guess.

REEGE: Well, don't be. As many of you know, Tara is our first contestant under the terms of a settlement ABC reached with the National Organization of Women. They filed a formal complaint with the EEOC about the number of women making it to the final rounds of our little game here, and ABC has asked me to announce that we are pleased with the progress of the negotiations. Oh, and for those of you watching at home, next week's contestant, a deaf mulatto lesbian dwarf, is already here in the audience. Let's give her a round of applause.

[Cue audience applause as small, brown hand reaches up from behind seat to sign "Thanks, Reege."]

REEGE: You're welcome! Now, Tara, here's your first question on Who Wants To Be A Limousine Liberal? [Brief applause]: A church member is excommunicated for publicly criticizing his faith's teachings on homosexuality. As a limousine liberal, should you support or oppose this parishioner's excommunication?

204

TARA: Well, I think it's certainly wrong for Catholics who accept homosexuality to be punished for affirming the gay lifestyle, and I don't think the church has the right to suppress unpopular opinions, so as a liberal, I oppose the excommunication.

REEGE: Is that your...final answer?

TARA: Yes, Reege, it is.

REEGE: I'm so sorry, Tara, but excommunication is the liberal's answer.

[Audience groan. Play dirge-like "You're a Loser" music]

Yes, Tara, the man kicked out of the very liberal Episcopal Church USA was anti-homosexuality activist Lewis Green of Asheville, North Carolina. He was banned from church property and denied the sacraments because he publicly opposed the church's pro-homosexuality policies. Therefore, the right answer for a limousine liberal is: Ban the [bleep].

[Audience laughter; more music]

TARA: Does this mean I lose?

REEGE: Oh, no, Tara. Nobody loses on "Who Wants To Be a Limousine Liberal?" We believe in building self-esteem. Plus, our legal settlement with NOW gives you five more chances to win!

TARA: But there are only four more questions...

REEGE: Wow! Math must really be your subject, Tara! Now let's go to the next question. Tara, as a liberal, would you support or oppose investigating the personal, sexual lives of political figures and using that information to attack their careers?

TARA: I think what happened to President Clinton was awful! Those mean-spirited Republicans were on a sexual witch-hunt that was unfair

205

and unnecessary, and besides, I think Bill Clinton is cute. I'd do him! [Giggles, laughter from audience]

So digging up dirt on people's sex lives is not a liberal thing to do. That's my final answer.

REEGE: Well, Tara, I'm afraid you're wrong again! It was Clinton-ally Tina Brown who paid $100,000 for a book outing homosexual staff members in Ken Starr's office and revealing the personal sex lives of anti-Clinton journalists. I guess Kathie Lee's glad Frank got out of broadcasting! [Laughter, more music.]

Now let's go to taxes. Tara, is it liberal to support regressive taxes that transfer money from poor, black neighborhoods to affluent, white suburbs?

TARA: Oh, that's a hard one. Can I use a lifeline? I'd like to call Democrat Governor Jim Hodges of South Carolina.

REEGE: Okay. AT&T, connect us to the Governor's Mansion in Columbia, South Carolina.

[Sound of phone picking up]

GOVERNOR: Huh? Hello?

REEGE: Governor Hodges, this is Regis.

GOVERNOR: Regis! How are ya, buddy? You tell that fine South Carolinian, Vanna White, I said "Hi."

REEGE: Wrong show, Governor. Anyway, Tara is here with a question: Does a good liberal support regressive taxes that take from the urban poor and give to the suburban rich?

HODGES: They do if they wanna get re-elected, Tara. It's called the lottery!

TARA: I don't know. That still doesn't sound very liberal to me. We're supposed to help poor people.

REEGE: Oh! I'm so sorry, Tara. This just doesn't seem to be your night. Liberals love the lottery because the money goes to help liberals! But don't worry, we've still got the big money lightning round. I'll give you the ideological position, and you tell me if it's conservative or liberal. Set the clock. Okay. Go. [Ticking clock begins.]

REEGE: Laws that treat people differently based on race.

TARA: Racist laws? That's not liberal. [Buzzer]

REEGE: Sorry, that's wrong. Have you forgotten affirmative action? Next: Businesses using their advertising clout to keep unpopular opinions off the airwaves?

TARA: Censorship? I'm against that, right?

REEGE: Too bad, Tara. I've got two words for you: Dr. Laura. [Buzzer]

Well, Tara, time's up for tonight. The bad news is, you missed every single question. The good news is that the questions have been deemed inherently sexist by our judges, so you are declared the winner by default!

So congratulations, Tara, and good night, everybody! This is your ol' buddy Reege reminding you that, in the world of American liberalism, losers are always the big winners!

My Life As A Fashion Plate

April, 2000

"A vain man can never be utterly ruthless; he wants to win applause and therefore accommodates himself to others." — *Goethe*

Through a series of coincidences, I have appeared on national television a dozen times or so in the past year. Being a media minor-leaguer, it's always flattering and exciting to play "talking head" with the big boys — my ideas, my opinions being bandied about on TV screens across the nation, influencing the media elite in New York, Washington, perhaps even the White House.

Think about it: I, Michael Graham, lowly graduate of Pelion High, now a cable-network Cicero shaping the intellectual discourse of our great nation! And the reaction back home?

"Don't you own a tie?"

The first call, the first accolade from a friend back home after my debut on ABC's *Politically Incorrect*, and the very first comment out of his mouth is about my *wardrobe*?

Sure, I own a tie, I told him. But I hate wearing ties and it's a late-night talk show, and I was wearing a sports coat, and anyway what I really wanted to know was what he thought of the devastating volley of sparkling witticisms I launched at the Clinton administration.

"Yeah, fine, right," he shrugged, "But Michael — the clothes! Jeans, sneakers, no tie? You looked like you were teaching a freshman English class at a technical college. You're on national TV for chrissake. Next time, wear a tie."

This was particularly galling to me for two reasons. First, because the comments came from a friend who is both active in conservative politics and a heterosexual, which means A) he should have been interested in what I had to say, and B) he doesn't have any better taste in clothes than I do.

Secondly, my life as a clotheshorse and fashion plate has been an utter disaster. I was a fat kid growing up and was forced to wear clothes from the "Husky" section of Sears, which means they were made by unskilled laborers out of materials found in the store. What passed for a pair of pants bore a suspicious resemblance to a pup tent on sale the week before.

As I grew older, my fashion failings continued. I honestly believe that the day the leisure suit went from a symbol of '70s style to a wardrobe punchline was the day I showed up at Pelion High in a brand-new powder blue model with lapels the size of an interstate off ramp.

At Oral Roberts University, my dislike for dress clothes may have been aggravated by the campus dress code. Being forced to wear a tie to class every day was bad enough. The fact that my entire collection of neckware consisted of those square-ended knit ties that were fashionable for about 45 minutes during the early days of the Reagan administration just made it worse.

I should point out that I purchased none of these clothes for myself. Every item of clothing I have purchased in my lifetime could fit in a single dresser drawer at a Motel 6, with room left over for the Gideon Bible. Like almost every man, I only own clothes that women have bought for me. I wear them without question, the same way a prisoner wears his bright orange jumpsuit. Does it look stupid? Sure, but what am I supposed to do about it?

So when ABC called, the last thing on my mind was my wardrobe. But instead of winning praise for my insightful comments or clever repartee, I flunked the fashion test.

And my conservative friend's critique was only the beginning. Not only did I get more snide comments about my wardrobe on *P.I.*, but the same thing happened after every subsequent television appearance, too. Every guest shot on C-SPAN or MSNBC would be followed by a steady stream of criticisms from friends, family, ideological fellow-travelers, all of them suddenly transformed into faux Ralph Laurens: Couldn't they do something to your hair? They let you wear jeans? Why the sports coats? Don't you own a suit? Were those really white athletic socks you had on?

Wait a minute, I interrupted, as one friend laid out his clothing critique. You mean you can't remember anything I said about the Republican presidential primary, but you noticed what color my *socks* were?

"How could I miss them? Straight out of gym class. Jeez, Michael, who wears tube socks on national television?"

Now, I could get defensive and point out that David Letterman in fact wears sneakers on his show every night. I could also argue that as a humor writer and radio talk host, I should utilize my wardrobe to highlight my hip, happenin', counter-culture role as an irreverent media gadfly of the entrenched political establishment. Kind of a John McCain-type if John McCain didn't want to beat the crap out of Pat Robertson.

Yes, I could make these arguments and, in fact I did, but to no avail. When I mentioned creating a Michael Graham "look," my friends just laughed. "You already have a look: Geeky White Republican. Now lace up your wingtips, button down your collar and shut up."

Mel Gibson can wear a black T-shirt with his gray business suit because he's Mel Gibson — movie star. Woody Allen can show up for an interview in a ratty sweater and beat-up corduroys because he's Woody Allen — cradle-robber. And Jennifer Lopez can attend the Grammy Awards (almost) wearing a decorative shower curtain and a swatch of gauze because — well, because she is so incredibly hot. But me? I can't catch a break.

I've learned my lesson. I'll be back on TV soon and, though I haven't a clue as to what the topic is or who the guests will be, please tune in:

I've got a handmade silk tie that is to die for.

It Is...

It is the only gift you will get this Christmas. And it is the only one you will give.

It is why a pair of socks wrapped in green paper sounds so much like a dinosaur when shaken by a small boy.

It is a middle-aged man, teeth gritted and face darkly red, trying to remain nonchalant as a nubile young sales lady holds up two lacy undergarments and asks him to guess which one will fit his wife.

It is what makes him answer: "The small one."

It is the vaccination protecting a child's belief in Santa from the sound of familiar voices in the attic on Christmas Eve.

It is the meaning of the word "Pokemon" in a 7-year-old's bedtime prayer.

It is the scent of a crib warmed by a sleeping baby. It is the accompanying memory loss that makes a mother of teen-aged children lean over that crib and wish she could do it again.

It is why this mother believes any future children would be intelligent, respectful and pleasant.

It is why the street person's hunger makes him sad instead of angry. And why the five-dollar bill you hurriedly shove into his shaking hand will be spent on a single Big Mac and a 12-pack of Milwaukee's Finest.

It is the only reason a married man shaves before coming to bed.

It is what makes his wife believe he's just trying to improve his personal hygiene.

It is the sudden, listening stillness of a woman's kitchen at Christmastime when she hears the screen door latch, even though he hasn't come home in years.

211

It's what turns the dollar-store, slave-labor, nylon-haired knock-off into a Ballerina Barbie when touched by her 6-year-old fingers.

It's what makes her father blink back a tear and silently promise to give her a real Christmas next year.

It is why he can't remember making the same promise when she was five.

It is the unexplainable meteorological phenomenon that puts the feel of coming snow in the air each Christmas Eve, even in South Carolina. It's what presses small noses to window panes at bedtime, and causes you to tune in the local weatherman at 11 p.m..... just to make sure.

It is why we can't imagine Christmas dinner without Gramma, and why Gramma sometimes looks up with a start when she hears her name. It's why she thought, just for a moment, that it was her mother calling.

It is why she isn't sure that it wasn't.

It is the sole motivator for your sister to ever touch an oven. Especially after what happened last year.

It is the reason you really, honestly thought you were going to eat that piece of fruitcake when you cut it.

And when she has put your children to bed, stuffed the last bit of wrapping paper into a closet, taken the potpourri off the stove, turned out all the lights in your house and finally falls onto the sofa next to you — as you sit quietly with her before the glistening tree — it is the only thing that can convince you that she might love you half as much as you love her.

It is why she does.

It is the reason women weep. It is the reason men fail. It is why every child, at least once in his life, has wanted to cry at Christmas.

It is as precious as a baby, wrapped in swaddling clothes and lying in a manger. It is as painful as a flesh-torn hand and a thorn-crowned head. It is the reason for both.

And if every Santa song and earnest prayer, every sincere gift and imagined wrong, every Christmas dinner and New Year's toast, every unanswered invitation and unwelcome guest, every office party kiss and happy child's hug — if every human moment of the entire holiday season — could be stripped of its tinsel and pretense and price tag and reduced to its truest essence, we would find it there, the only one gift ever given at Christmas, the same gift, passed from hand to hand.

It is hope.

It is Christmas.

AFTERWORD

To the American People
Tuesday, November 5th, 2024
Election Day

My fellow, future Americans:

You are reading this modest collection of late-20th-century reminiscences on a day in my not-too-distant future. Many of the events recounted herein will be dimmed, perhaps even lost, before your time.

But as you prepare for this momentous day—Election Day—in the year 2024, I am confident that you will still feel the effects of the decisions that we, the Americans of 2000, made in your stead more than 20 years earlier.

Today, you are watching history in the making as William Jefferson Clinton—an active, healthy, though somewhat hefty man of 78—stands on the eve of a victorious political campaign for his third non-consecutive term as president of the United States. As you look excitedly toward the future under the Clinton/(Mary) Cheney ticket, I hope you find time to also think of us, the generation that gave you this man and his legacy.

We were the generation of Americans who held President Clinton's fate in our hands. If, back in the 1990s, we had not nurtured him, encouraged him, forgiven him and fostered his dreams of a felony-conviction-free future, there would be no Bill Clinton for you today.

215

There wouldn't have been the Clinton/Buchanan administration of 2009-2017, to ride (and perhaps reign in) the surge of American nationalism after Mexico unilaterally annexed itself into our 51-55th states. If not for President "America First!" Clinton's uniquely flexible political philosophy, our country might not have survived the turmoil.

And now, in 2024, when our nation needs them most, Bill Clinton and his lovely new bride, Mrs. Pamela Anderson Lee Clinton, are ready to serve once again. It is disturbing to think of the many times along the way when a single stumble could have denied us the leadership of this great man:

What if the truth about his draft record had come out before New Hampshire? If the truth of the Chinese campaign finance story had surfaced before the '96 elections? If Ken Starr had granted Monica Lewinsky immunity in January of 1998 instead of July? If the second Independent Council, Robert Ray, hadn't mysteriously committed suicide with Vince Foster's gun just days before bringing criminal charges against President Clinton? If that Chinese missile hadn't missed the sorority house where the President was staying the night WWIII broke out?

We could have lost the President at any of those moments, or in hundreds of others in the national thrill ride that is the Clinton life story. But we didn't; we hung on. We, the people of America in the last century, we simply could not let go.

There were moments we were sorely tempted, tempted to look past a president who was a mirror of ourselves. Some said we should look beyond the reflection of Bill Clinton and toward our better selves. We occasionally longed to be a better America, a nation of courageous people who, through self-sacrifice and effort would lift ourselves beyond our immediate emotions and desires... but then "Survivor" came on and we forgot about it.

But happily, there was Bill Clinton, always willing to take us back into his welcoming, unquestioning arms. He loved us—or at least craved our love—just the way we are.

If there is one lesson we have learned in our time that we could share with you, the Americans of our future, it is this: Bill Clinton isn't just an American. He *is* America. He is at once both our fanciful vision of ourselves and an embodiment of who we truly are.

To leave him behind would mean so much more than a change in political parties. It would be to change ourselves, to change our character, to accept the fact that life is frequently difficult, that to be an adult means the deferment of juvenile desires, that our character is not revealed in our intentions, but in our actions.

The American people are not ready to accept that, and neither is Bill Clinton. And as long as we both have each other, we won't have to.

God bless you, and God bless Bill Clinton's United States of America.